THE LINCOLN BRIGADE

A Picture History

SECOND EDITION

By William Loren Katz and Marc Crawford
illustrated with photographs

Preface by Robin D. G. Kelley

The Apex Press

*This book is respectfully dedicated
to the Americans who fought
to save democracy in Spain
and to warn of
the Nazi danger.*

Map from *The Lincoln Brigade* by Edwin Rolf, 1939, reprinted by permission of Random House, New York 6. Abraham Lincoln Brigade Archive/Brandeis University 24, 29, 36, 38a, 38b, 39, 41a, 41b, 47, 48a, 49, 50, 51, 52, 53b, 54, 55, 56, 57, 58, 64, 66, 67, 68, 69a, 69b, 73, 74-5, 77, 78a, 78b. George Watt 8. Joe Whelan 30b, 34-35, 37b, 43, 45b, 46a, 59a. Sam Walters Title page, 7, 27, 30, 33, 44, 45a, 46, 90. Magnum Photos, Robert Capa 10-11, 12, 70. David Seymour 14. William Loren Katz 16a, 36, 48b, 61b, 78b, 85a, 85b, 88. RCMS Photo 16b. Library of Congress 17, 19a, 19b, 20, 59b, 62. Steve Nelson 21, 42, 65. Morris Brier 22, 23. Moe Fishman 86. Harry Hakim 28, 31, 53a. James Yates 32, 37a, 40. Milton Wolff 72. Paul Robeson Archieves 61a. New York Public Library 76. Robert Coane 82, 83, 84. Abby Lane 81, 86, back cover.

© 1989 and 2001 Ethrac Publications, Inc.

Second Edition published by The Apex Press, an imprint of the Council on International and Public Affairs, Suite 3C, 777 United Nations Plaza, New York, NY 10017 (800-316-2739) www.cipa-apex.org

Title page photo: Lincoln Brigade attacks Villanueva de la Canada, led by Capt. Oliver Law, in uniform, third from right. (Photo: Sam Walters)

Contents

Langston Hughes interviews volunteer Crawford Morgan.

Preface

*F*or the past fifteen years, I've taught a variety of 20th century history courses at the undergraduate and graduate level. And every year, without exception, one question stumps all of my students: "When did American soldiers first enter the Second World War?" "1941! After the Japanese invaded Pearl Harbor!" they shouted, often in a self-congratulatory tone. And yet, a more careful assessment of World War II's origins suggests that they were off by about five years.

If we understand World War II as a global struggle against fascism, I'd argue, then the conflict begins in Spain in 1936 with General Franciso's Franco's army mutiny against the democratically elected Republican government. It is called a "Civil War," but this is really a misnomer. Without support from Mussolini's Italy, Hitler's Germany, and Portugal under the dictatorship of Antonio de Oliveira Salazar, Franco and his rebel troops could not have succeeded. Military and material aid shifted the balance of power, and the Western democracies' decision to stay neutral and impose an embargo on the Republic contributed to the unequal balance of power. Only the Soviet Union and Mexico officially came to the aid of the Republic.

My students generally know nothing about the Spanish Civil War, but they follow my line of reasoning and some are persuaded. But when I tell them that nearly 3,000 Americans traveled to Spain to defend the Republican government from fascist forces, and that they were joined by another 35,000 volunteers from around the globe, that is when I lose them. Most stare at me in utter disbelief. They cannot fathom why anyone in their right mind would travel half way across the world to fight, and possibly die, for a country that is not theirs. And for no money! My more activist-oriented students are delighted to discover such a significant episode of international solidarity. Before learning of the Lincohn Brigade, they were convinced that theirs was the first generation to attempt to organize on such a global scale.

Every year I teach the story of the Spanish Civil War and the heroic participation of the International Brigades because it represents perhaps the greatest example of internationalism in the 20th century. The brigadistas volunteered not to defend one country but to defend humanity; they honestly believed that old labor slogan, "an injury to one is an injury to all." Their story ought to be common knowledge, but just try to find a high school student who has heard of the Spanish Civil War. We should not be too surprised by this sad state of affairs. The role Americans played in the fight to defend Spanish democracy was more than "forgotten"; it was consciously erased from our collective memory.

Cold Warriors tried their best to turn a noble example of democratic liberalism into a vile act of subversion, and when that failed, history textbooks and social science teachers simply ignored the Lincoln Brigade. Why? Because those who volunteered were labelled subversives—they were "premature antifascists." Many were, in fact, Communists and independent radicals, but their greatest crime was to fight fascism on Spanish soil before our nation's leaders were prepared to go to battle.

Thanks to this new edition of *The Lincoln Brigade,* we have a chance to reach more people with this remarkable story. This narrative will take you directly to the horrifying front lines of Jarama, across the jagged Pyrennese mountains, and back and forth into the contested streets and farms of America, where the Lincoln's commitment to social justice was born. It is the extraordinary story of ordinary working people—people who, for the most part, had never traveled outside the country—risking their lives for the cause of liberty. They demonstrate that internationalism is not the preserve of those we call "intellectuals," that assembly line workers, nurses and sharecroppers are capable of seeing their own struggles tied to working people throughout the world. What an astonishing example for current and future generations!

Best of all, these men and women never quit. They returned home, as this updated edition of *The Lincoln Brigade* shows, to continue the good fight—battling Nazism in World War II, opposing U.S. racism and military interventions in the Americas, reaching out to Franco's political prisoners, working for the liberation of South Africa and Nelson Mandela—and still marching in 2000, this time to demand the removal of a U.S. Navy that uses Vieques, Puerto Rico, as a military firing range.

So study these fine photos in all their detail, the glowing, determined faces of arrivals, Oliver Law's hip beret, the bearded and shirtless kids who barely achieved manhood, the warm smiles of Evelyn Hutchins and Salaria Key, the wounded, fatigued, but resolute faces of returnees, the vigorous anti-fascist demonstrations that reach to the year 2000.

William Loren Katz and the late Marc Crawford have put together a richly detailed narrative and beautiful portrait of struggle and triumph, victory and defeat, and more struggle. Please read this book and circulate it. Read it aloud and spread this history like folklore and oral tradition. Make it part of our collective memory, our common story, our common knowledge. If we do, kids of all ages may very well hold up their fists, continue the good fight, and say to the IMF and World Bank, *"No Pasaran!"*

—Robin D. G. Kelley

6

Acknowledgments

*T*his project could not have been completed without the assistance of the Abraham Lincoln Brigade Archive/Brandeis University Spanish Civil War Collection and archivist Victor Berch; Mr. Cornell Capa and the Robert Capa Photograph Collection; New York University's Tamiment Library; the Resource Center for Marxist Studies; the Lincoln Brigade's Fiftieth Anniversary Tour of Spain; Sam Walters, Jim Yates, Joe Whelan, George Watt, Harry Hakim, Morris Brier, and Steve Nelson, who scoured their private collections for photographs; the Veterans of the Abraham Lincoln Brigade, particularly their commander, Steve Nelson, who provided advice and valuable leads; and also Leonard Lamb (who scrutinized military de-tails), Abe Smorodin, William Sussman, Charles Nusser, Moe Fishman, Jim Yates, and others in the New York office, and Dr. William Pike, Harry Fisher, Bill Bailey, Hilda Roberts, Milton Wolff, and dozens of other veterans who were interviewed; and photographers Abby London and Robert Coane. To have traveled through Spain in October 1986 with these unwarlike souls was an experience to be savored and never forgotten.

For helping turn this revised edition into a virtually new book, the author wishes to thank the following individuals: Moe Fishman; Harry Fisher; Tibby Brooks, curator of the Sam Walters collection; and Abby London Crawford.

Lincoln and other International Brigaders at rest.

Ernest Hemingway *(right)* with Captain Milton Wolff, the twenty-two-year old art student who served as the last commander of the Lincoln Battalion in Spain. Hemingway described Wolff as "tall as Lincoln, and as brave and as good a soldier as any that commanded battalions at Gettysburg." George Watt is on the extreme left.

Introduction

During the Spanish civil war (1936-39) some twenty-eight hundred enthusiastic young American men and women left home to help save the republic of Spain from a military take-over. Joined by thirty-five thousand volunteers from fifty-two other countries, they formed a unique army. It was the only time in history a global volunteer force assembled to fight for an ideal—democracy. In a prelude to World War II, these young people battled armies dispatched by the Fascist dictators Hitler and Mussolini. The U.S. volunteers were the youngest, with the least combat experience. The artists, poets, and visionaries among them outnumbered trained soldiers.

The gallantry of these volunteers from many nations did not move leading democratic governments to help, but it influenced artists the world the world over. It inspired Picasso's celebrated painting *Guernica*, and such classic modern novels as Ernest Hemingway's *For Whom the Bell Tolls* and Andre Malraux's *Man's Hope*. It sent a shock wave to a generation of young writers on both sides of the Atlantic: George Orwell, Stephen Spender, W. H. Auden, John Dos Passos, Langston Hughes, and Pablo Neruda. More books were written about Spain's early skirmish with facism than about all of World War I.

The story of the U.S. contingent, though part of America's national heritage, has not found its way into many schoolbooks or history courses. This means few know that their fellow citizens took up arms against Hitler and Mussolini before Pearl Harbor – or that these unusual Americans fought in the first U.S. armed force that was racially integrated from top to bottom.

Rarely more than a battalion in actual strength during any battle, they have been traditionally called the Abraham Lincoln Brigade.

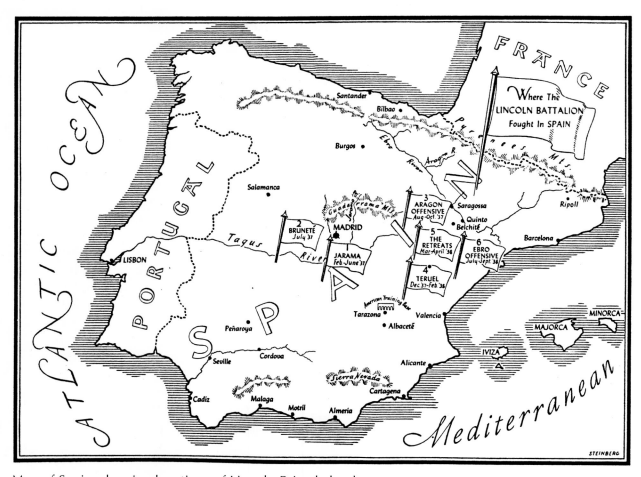

Map of Spain, showing locations of Lincoln Brigade battles.

Right: Volunteers from many nations on their way to the front in Madrid in 1936.

Part I

Sounds from Distant Battle

The most famous photo of the war was taken by Robert Capa from a trench—a republican soldier at the moment of death.

ONE

"They Shall Not Pass!"

*I*n 1936, the new democracy in Spain was fighting for its life. For fifteen centuries Spain had been ruled by a backward monarchy. Then, in forty-eight hours, in 1931, it bloodlessly replaced a king with a republic. A weak and divided new government had to battle its past rulers—rich landlords and aristocratic officers supported by a powerful church. The democracy tried mightily to feed its hungry, raise wages, create a public school system, separate church and state, and begin reforms, while the old rulers began to plot a return.

There was turmoil and violence in the countryside as landless peasants and landlords fought for control. A battle for equality exploded in cities. Women began to assert rights to divorce and property, and to wear trousers. "Madrid is a madhouse," said a European visitor. "Every man, woman, and child has gone crazy. They cannot have always been like this. The waiters . . . will not take tips; every man is his fellow's equal."

Landlords and army generals had not given up the fight for power. In villages their civil guards arrested peasant leaders, broke strikes, and tortured prisoners. The aristocrats drew strength from fascism's rise in Europe. Some plotted with Mussolini for a return of the monarchy. Others saw Hitler as an ally.

On February 16, 1936, a Popular Front alliance of parties won the election. The ancient ruling class of Spain had been decisively defeated. But now it began a vast military conspiracy.

Spain's top generals plotted a rebellion, and on July 18, 1936, they seized weapons in Morocco to overthrow the republic. The generals won support from Germany, Italy, and the dictatorship in nearby Portugal. By early August, forty Nazi and Fascist cargo and bomber planes were ferrying rebel General Francisco Franco's armies from Morocco to Seville. By October rebel trucks, with Nazi planes overhead, rolled toward Madrid and—the rebels and everyone else believed—a quick victory.

Civil wars can be brutal, and this one was among the worst. Franco's forces murdered prisoners, republican sympathizers, and occasionally the enemy wounded. They forced peasant sons into their army. Picking up Nazi ideas, rebel General Queipo de Llano proclaimed by radio in October that Franco was fighting "a war of Western civilization against the Jews of the world."

To counter outside Fascist intervention, republican Spain asked the world for help. Radio Barcelona broadcast this call:

> Workers and anti-Fascists of all lands! We the workers of Spain are poor but we are pursuing a noble ideal. Our fight is your fight. Our victory

is the victory of liberty. We are the vanguard of the international proletariat in the fight against fascism. Men and women of all lands! Come to our aid!

Hundreds of volunteers began to pour over the Pyrenees. Some early arrivals from neighboring France were hard-drinking veterans of World War I. They had little respect for Spain's customs or its women and had to be sent back home.

Then a new kind of dedicated soldier arrived. By early November two thousand were in Madrid's first International Brigade. The original force was made up of German refugees, British machine gunners, an author, a nephew of Winston Churchill, and Pietro Nenni, once Musolini's friend. Some had even escaped from concentration camps in Germany and from imprisonment in Italy to fight Hitler and Mussolini in Spain. U.S. writer John Dos Passos described these refugees:"…a feeling of energy and desperation comes from them. The dictators have stolen their world from them; they have lost their home, their families, their hopes of a living or a career; they are fighting back."

Madrid's workers voted in union meetings to organize military columns. So did political groups. Children and women helped build barricades, and women ran the quartermaster corps. A battalion of Spanish women guarded the Segovia bridge. Delores Ibarruri, elected to Parliament, became La Pasionaria, the voice of resistant Spain. Her voice blared from Madrid radios, "It is better to die on your feet than to live on your knees! *No pasaran* (They shall not pass)!" Facing rebel armies at the gates of Madrid were people in work clothes, armed with lunch and rifles. Their motto, *No pasaran,* became Spain's slogan.

The courage of Madrid inspired intellectuals. Author George Orwell said Spain repre-

Members of the Thaelmann Column escaped from Nazi Germany to fight fascism in Spain.

sented "a thrill of hope. For here at last, apparently, was democracy standing up to fascism." Arriving as a reporter, Orwell joined a Barcelona militia. The famous French author André Malraux arrived with two old bombers and a few pilots. With some more old World War I planes and pilots, he organized Spain's first air force.

Germans, Italians, Belgians, Poles, Hungarians, Jews, Slavs, Britons, and Irish stood alongside the men and women of Madrid. Some had been drafted in World War I, while others had been draft evaders. Now they had proudly picked their army and war.

General Franco and his Fascist allies had not counted on Madrid's resistant spirit, and neither had anyone else. Rebel General Mola boasted the city would be taken by his four columns, and by "a fifth column" inside. He said he would have coffee in Madrid on October 12, a national holiday. Madrid held out; his coffee grew cold. Radio Lisbon broadcast news of a triumphant General Franco riding into a defeated Madrid on a white charger. Germany and Italy announced Franco would be given official recognition when he captured the city. They had to make other plans.

Spain's civilian army in home-stitched uniforms handed world fascism its first defeat. With old rifles-often one to every three soldiers-they halted some of Europe's best-trained armies in front of Madrid. Spain's citizens learned they could fight, and more, they discovered they were not alone.

The first Americans reached Spain long before a Lincoln Battalion was formed. Carmelo Delgado, twenty-three, a Puerto Rican, was one of nine children born to a poor Guayama family. He shared an unheated Madrid room with two other students. Then Delgado helped form a troop to protect the city. He was captured and executed. Other early U.S. volunteers included an Italian-American editor, a jewish engineer, and athletes from an anti-Nazi Olympics in Barcelona. Stephen Dudak became the first U.S. airman in Spain and the first to shoot down a German Heinkel. In early 1937, when the U.S. had only five licensed black pilots, two, James Peck and Paul Williams, arrived. Peck brought down two German Heinkels and three Italian Fiats to become Spain's fourth-ranking U.S. ace. By the time Spain was able to rely on its own airmen, in November, U.S. pilots had brought down forty-eight enemy planes.

While volunteers poured into Spain from

Women take rifle practice before joining the front lines in Madrid.

¿QUE HACES TU PARA

EVITAR ESTO?

AYUDA A MADRID

This poster issued by republican Spain's Ministry of Propaganda portrayed the horrors endured by civilians bombed by Nazi and Fascist planes.

phone exchange at British Gibraltar to keep in contact with Berlin, Rome, and Lisbon. "I hope they send in enough Germans to finish the war," the British ambassador to Spain told the U.S. ambassador.

American policy followed that of the British. The U.S. even supplied most of Franco's oil. In July, five Texas Oil Company tankers bound for republican Spain were directed to rebel ports. Four-fifths of rebel trucks came from General Motors, Studebaker, and Ford. The Texas Oil Company, increasing the amount each year, sold Franco 1,856,000 tons of oil in all. The U.S. State Department made travel to Spain illegal in January 1937 and once even tried to prevent U.S. doctors, nurses, and medical supplies from reaching the embattled republic. Franco's world credit was so strong he never had to borrow money.

By October 1936, the USSR and Mexico decided to help the republic. But Mexico was too poor and far away, and the USSR had to send ships through submarine packs at sea and penetrate closed land borders.

Volunteers from all over traveled to Spain by an illegal underground railroad. Its main office, in Paris, was directed by Josip Broz—who later became President Tito of Yugoslavia. European governments tried to halt it. Switzerland made talk about the civil war illegal, Scandinavian countries passed laws against travel to Spain, and Belgium asked fifteen years in prison for anyone trying to reach Spain. But nothing stopped the flow.

everywhere, the United States government and democratic governments in Europe did nothing to help. France, on England's demand, closed its border to Spain in August. England and France feared a war with Germany, and they didn't want it to start in Spain. Their governments also had high officials who approved of Hitler and believed he would fight against communism, not against democracy. England's "Nonintervention Committee" enlisted twenty-six countries in a program to block aid to Spain's legal government, but allowed Hitler and Mussolini to aid the rebels. It permitted the rebels to use the tele-

Political cartoons, such as this one by William Gropper, which appeared on September 4, 1936, alerted some citizens to the fight in Spain.

SUPPORT PEOPLE'S FRONT SPAIN

16

TWO

The Great Depression

The American volunteers who left for Spain were reacting to two events—the Great Depression at home and the rise of fascism abroad. In the 1930s the Depression, the world's greatest economic disaster, gave citizens time to think and a lot to think about. By 1932 an estimated fourteen million U.S. wage earners were walking the streets. Banks and businesses collapsed, so many families without jobs also lost their savings.

Hungry children cried themselves to sleep and worried parents wondered how to feed their families, how to pay the rent. Farm families who could not meet their bank payments were forced from their farms. City tenants, unable to pay the rent, were evicted from their homes, and many had to move in with relatives. Some families lived on vacant lots, in homes made from cardboard boxes and wooden crates.

The American dream had turned into a nightmare. People stood in long lines for lukewarm soup. On street corners World War I veterans sold apples. Children were unable to attend school because they lacked warm clothes or shoes. Mothers and children sometimes poked through piles of garbage, searching for something to wear, to sell, to eat. Some people broke into stores to seize cans of food, bread, and veg-

Hunger marchers, organized by unemployment councils, reached Washington, D.C., on December 6, 1931. They demanded unemployment insurance from Congress.

etables. So many young people left home for the open road, it seemed half the country was hitching a ride to the other half.

Suicides and divorces doubled. When the Soviet Union advertised for workers, 100,000 unemployed U.S. citizens applied.

The U.S. volunteers who went to Spain had first battled against the hard times at home. They had helped move evicted families and their furniture back into their houses or apartments. They had helped hungry people get home relief payments. Some had organized marches demanding jobs, unemployment insurance, and social security. Many had tried to elect officials pledged to aid victims of the hard times.

Unemployment drove some desperate citizens to line up behind would-be dictators. Confused, angry men clustered in streets or in parks talking about the need for a Mussolini or Hitler to take command. Some joined hate groups such as the new Silver Shirts, the Christian Front, or the old Ku Klux Klan. These groups blamed minorities for the hard times, shouted Fascist slogans, and trained for military action. With Nazi swastikas flying, the German American Bund drilled with guns in New Jersey, rented New York's Madison Square Garden for huge rallies, and beat up Jews on the streets of New York.

Those who volunteered for Spain were influenced by radical ideas that flowered during the Depression. Governing committees of the Methodist and Congregationalist churches called capitalism "unchristian, unethical and antisocial," and one in four ministers in 1934 favored socialism. Once people laughed at Marxist views. Now they echoed with an American twang in bars, factories, and unions. Communism became a rising force. Party members talked endlessly and organized neighborhood protests and large demonstrations politicians could not ignore. They became heroes to many.

The Great Depression and the rise of Hitler had given a new spirit to American communism, which had been a tiny, rigid, and persecuted sect. By 1936 the party opened its doors wide: "We would grab anybody who attended two meetings, one if you were black," recalled Abe Smorodin. People lined up to sign up at outdoor meetings. Many of the communists who went to Spain had been enrolled in the youth division—the Young Communist League. The YCL fielded a softball team in Manhattan and ran a social and athletic club in Brooklyn. It was known for the interesting, attractive young people at its many socials. They had joined to fight poverty, injustice, and fascism's threat to the world.

Moe Fishman, a YCL member from New York, recalls he "was told I could go to Spain if I recruited ten others. I did, but none showed up except me. And what kind of Communists were we?" he asked. "We knew next to nothing about Marxism….I was a member for three years, so I knew a lot." He laughed. Arthur Landis, nineteen, signed up for Spain after "reading, attending meetings, campaigns, picket lines, unemployment demonstrations—all things required of a starry-eyed youth. Spain was everywhere, on everyone's lips, in every newspaper."

Government officials, indifferent to the human pain of the hard times, often drove citizens toward the Communist party and other radical groups. President Hoover infuriated many by claiming "prosperity is just around the corner." Hoover ordered the U.S. Army to disperse fifteen thousand veterans who had marched into and camped in Washington to demand a promised bonus. In the summer of 1932, "General MacArthur opened fire on the veterans." Rosario Piston was shocked.

Then, in December, Vice President Charles Curtis greeted a delegation representing three thousand starving marchers with: "You just hand me your petition. You needn't make any speech. I have only a few minutes' time."

At Christmas, Carl Geiser, an Ohio college

Communist march in Pittsburgh, Pennsylvania, to demand work and relief, around 1932-34.

U.S. troops besiege the camp of the Bonus Expeditionary Force in Washington, D.C., on July 28, 1932, using tear gas and guns. President Hoover ordered the attack, and General Douglas MacArthur carried it out with officers Dwight David Eisenhower and George Patton.

student, was raising money for a Congress Against War and Fascism. He approached World War I Secretary of War Newton Baker and was told: "Maybe we need a little war to get rid of some of the unemployed." Pistone and Geiser went to Spain.

President Franklin D. Roosevelt had been elected in 1932, and his policies, called the New Deal, handed out relief and enacted reforms. There were ten million still jobless and more in distress in 1936 when he ran for reelection and captured forty-six of forty-eight states. People's fear of a dictatorship by the rich faded, and for the first time in years citizens who had been worried about problems at home relaxed and took a fresh look at the world.

They were just in time. In November, Italy, Germany, and Japan completed the Axis military pact. Its announced aim was to "save Western civilization from communism." But Hitler privately declared the Axis would defeat communism and the Western posers, and predicted: "In three years Germany will be ready."

The Axis alliance was only the latest piece of terrifying news from Europe and Asia. Fascist dictators ruled Germany, Italy, and Japan, and had a foothold in Bulgaria, Hungary, Lithuania, Greece, Poland, Rumania, and Yugoslavia. In Europe only England, France, Czechoslovakia, the Scandanavian countries and Spain still had free elections.

It became hard to ignore the frightening news from Nazi Germany and Fascist Italy. Brown Shirts in Germany and Black Shirts in Italy beat down political foes, smashed unions, and talked about conquering the world. By 1933, concentration camps, locking away those who spoke out, dotted the German landscape. Nazi storm troopers assaulted Jewish men, women, and children, and in 1935, Nazi Nuremburg laws eliminated Jewish rights to own businesses or to hold decent jobs or German citizenship. In 1931, Japan had invaded Manchuria.

Armed pro-Nazi gangs, often funded by Berlin, tested democracy's weaknesses in France, Austria, and Spain. Slowly fascism's opponents decided they had better unite against this threat, or free elections were doomed. This unified

Young Nazis in Germany gleefully prepare to burn books with "dangerous ideas."

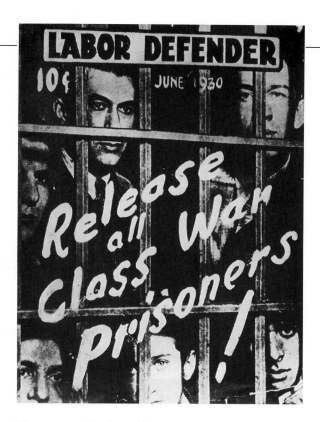

Steve Nelson *(top right)* and five others were jailed in 1930 in Chicago during protests for unemployment insurance.

stand against the danger of fascism called itself the Popular Front. The U.S. volunteers for Spain often worked for local Popular Front groups.

Hitler demonstrated his warlike intentions by marching his troops into the Rhineland on the border with France. He built a huge air force and announced an army of half a million. By 1936, Mussolini was completing an invasion of Ethiopia in Africa, where he launched history's first terror bombings of civilian populations.

Democratic governments responded to these threats with smiles and new offers. British and French officials who favored fascism secretly agreed to persuade Ethiopia to accept Italian domination. British Prime Minister Chamberlain conveyed to Hitler his acceptance of "alterations of the European order." By mentioning Austria, Czechoslovakia, and Danzig, he suggested that Germany march eastward, toward the USSR.

Then, a week after Roosevelt's reelection, there was the exciting news from Madrid, where citizens had stopped armies aided by Hitler and Mussolini. The dictators, with all their firepower and air superiority, had suffered defeat at the hands of ordinary Spaniards and a few thousand foreign volunteers.

Americans, emerging from the election, saw that Spain was in flames. Some saw a preview of another world war as Hitler practiced the blitzkrieg, or lightning war, in Spain. New planes, weapons, and techniques of warfare were being tested on Spain's civilians.

Steve Nelson and five others had been jailed in 1930 for demanding unemployment insurance. Since FDR was firmly in place and unemployment insurance was the law of the land, three of the six volunteered for Spain. They believed unless fascism was whipped once and for all, its storm troopers would march into one country after another. They believed that everyone, including the U.S., was in danger and "somebody had to do something."

THREE

Volunteers

Morris Brier of Brooklyn, New York, with Otto Reeves of Los Angeles, California, try to bring down an enemy plane in Spain.

*T*he idealistic men and women who volunteered to save the legal Spanish republican government represented an American cross-section. Most came from cities in large states, but they also included farmers and hillbillies. The largest group comprised members of trade unions, especially seamen. The second largest was made up of college students and professors. Dozens called themselves artists—writers, poets, painters, dancers, musicians, and three acrobats. There were Catholics, Protestants, Japanese, Chinese, Afro-Americans, and Native Americans. In the age of Hitler, Jews made up 30 percent of the Lincoln Brigade. There were Democrats, Republicans, Socialists, Communists, and people who rejected any kind of labels.

Hans Amlie was a Montana prospector and engineer. He saw men sent into mines "where silicosis was inevitable. Two years of work, one year of dying, and no compensation-that was their caree. I'd always fought for them, and so I lost job after job, for the owners got to know me. And then the war started. It was perfectly natural for me to come to Spain."

Three volunteers, Morris Brier, Otto Reeves, and Marc Haldane, became close friends in Spain. Reeves was the son of a black storefront minister in Cleveland. He graduated from high school and, not wanting to be a burden to his family, hitchhiked to California and worked for a University of Southern California fraternity. A white friend brought him to Communist meetings about the famous Scottsboro case. (Nine black youths had been framed in Scottsboro, Alabama, in 1931 for raping two white women, even though one of the women recanted her testimony in court.) Reeves began to read a lot, and in Spain he told Brier he wanted to test whether the Communists"who fought for black people . . . felt they were brothers and color did

22

not mean anything," and he wanted "to prove to myself that I am capable of risking my life for something I thought was correct."

Marc Haldane, son of a Native American chief in British Columbia, worked as a lumberjack and joined the Communist party. When he tried to unionize the lumbermen, he found himself blacklisted, unable to get a job. He thought his marksmanship could be useful in Spain.

Brier, Jewish and from Brownsville, Brooklyn, was one of many Communists who "never attended meetings." He and his friends took part in election campaigns, picketed for jobless relief, led rent strikes, and set up picket lines to force Woolworth to hire blacks. They often faced arrest. During a 1936 confrontation over an eviction, a policeman drew his pistol. According to Brier, fast action followed:

> We took his gun away and threw it down a sewer and fled. Up the winding stairs of the house we ran, the cops in pursuit, one firing his pistol. We jumped from one roof to another, and as I raced downstairs, a woman opened a door, pulled me in, and said, "Sit down, take off your jacket, you're my son." Her lie saved me from jail. From our group of about twenty-five that day, five of us went to Spain. I went because it was time for me to answer: "Was my mouth bigger than my feet?"

Bill Van Felix and Harry Fisher were part of a group of more than a dozen unpaid union organizers. For Van Felix, Spain "was one more battle of rich against poor." Fisher was inspired "by Spain's people standing up to Hitler as the world was going Fascist." He was one of fifteen volunteers who had grown up in New York Jewish orphan homes.

David Thompson was a professional writer who said: "Our government was not representing the will of the American people on the Spanish Civil War. And there was nothing you could do but do something personal. It was up to you. Put up or shut up. So a lot of guys went over there from all walks of life. . . . They were fighting for all the things we had, that America stood for."

Bill Bailey, a sailor, had helped form the National Maritime Union. Pathé newsreels of Germany educated him. "Every week you would see Nazi storm troopers burning books, jailing people, and laughing as they forced Jewish men and women on their knees to scrub streets with toothbrushes."

He concluded, "You have to do something to stir up people." On July 26, 1935, his chance came. The German ship *Bremen* berthed in New

Marc Haldane *(left)* in Spain with Morris Brier.

23

Nurse Salaria Key

York harbor, flying a swastika, welcoming visitors. Bailey "Low Life" McCormick, and a handful of other seamen went aboard as tourists. While his buddies battled the Nazi crew, the six-foot-two Bailey tried to rip down the swastika-"I would have eaten the thing to get it off"-and finally succeeded. One American was shot, and the others bloodied. Bailey was ready for Spain.

On August 31, 1935, Oliver Law, a Texas-born black Communist, helped organize a Chi-cago rally for Ethiopia. Despite a ban by Mayor Kelly, it drew ten thousand people and two thousand police. Law was the first speaker, and he suddenly appeared on a rooftop to address the crowd. By the time police arrested him, there was another speaker on another roof, and another . . . until six speakers were heard and arrested.

Ed Balchowsky, the only Jewish child in a midwestern community, felt he had to go: "I knew what oppression was. I had it all my life

24

when I was a kid. I wanted to go to help." Hilda Roberts left for Spain right after graduating from nursing school in Philadelphia: "I was someone who wanted to do something important with my life. I had no doubts.

Salaria Key, young and black, was moved by world events: "I'm not going to sit down and let this happen. I'm going to go out and help even if it means my life. This is my world. I'm a nurse."

Norman Perlman, born to a Socialist mother who was a dentist, volunteered because he was bored and wanted adventure. Vernon Brown, at nineteen a Wisconsin farmer, gave political reasons: "It was a matter of justice—the people voted in a republic and now they needed help saving it." Harry Wallach came from Pennsylvania farmlands: "I'm very patriotic. If someone invaded America, what would I do, sit back and let them? I decided to go." Ralph Field and his son John signed up together. Ralph had defied the Ku Klux Klan in Arkansas to help build a sharecroppers' union that united poor blacks and whites. Fritz Grell, a dispossessed Iowa farmer with a wife and six children, left with the hope that after a Republican victory he would settle his family in Spain.

Maury Colow, seventeen, was appalled when "Mussolini and his son-in-law described dropping bombs on Ethiopia as a beautiful sight." Colow and nine buddies met on a Brooklyn rooftop and agreed to volunteer together. Five would later die in Spain. His father sat on the board that passed him. "It tore at his heart to see his young son leave," Colow recalled.

Lenny Lamb volunteered. "If I'm really serious about making a new society in this world and in this country, I've got to be able to show that I can take it and can participate in the actual dirty work of building, of doing it."

Joe Whelan, from a poor Irish-American family, was a volunteer whose "parents had been born in the old country, so Europe was a part of us. I went to Spain to fight a gang-up of Hitler, the army, and church against the democracy."

UCLA student Hank Rubin said:

> I was quite liberal, but not radical. I supposed going was partly because I was Jewish, partly because I was writing a novel and this was the way to learn about life, partly because I was young and wanted to test myself, and partly because I had no ties.

John Kozar was a seaman who smuggled anti-Nazi pamphlets and guns into Germany in 1935. For this he was once arrested. Spain was an opportunity to fight again, armed this time.

More than a few, like Milt Cohen, quit college to go "just before graduation because I couldn't think about me at that point…but I had to be thinking about the world." Arriving in Paris to accept a ballet scholarship, Lester Gittleson sat in a theater and watched newsreels of rebel bombings in Spain. He volunteered.

Jim Yates slowly realized: "Ethiopia and Spain are our fight." He left Mississippi at sixteen to stand hungry and freezing in Chicago's Washington Park, listening to black and white radical speakers call for a march to Springfield for jobs. His life changed.

> Suddenly I felt as one with these people, black and white. I was part of their hopes, their dreams, and they were part of mine. And we were part of an even larger world of marching poor people. . . . We were millions. We couldn't lose. My throat swelled with pride. I sang loud enough for all of Chicago to hear.

At Springfield, National Guardsmen charged marchers from every angle. Yates saw whites and blacks helping each other to safety. "Tear gas clawed at my eyes," said Yates, and he saw "the power of the state."

During the Italian invasion of Ethiopia, Yates

helped collect food and handed out leaflets protesting the aggression. Unable to reach an Ethiopia that "always seemed to live in my blood," he discovered that "Spain couldn't have been a better example of the world I dreamed of. . . . How could I not volunteer?" He sailed on the *Ile de France* with three hundred others and climbed across the Pyrenees. Like almost all the volunteers, he had never fired a gun.

Vincent Lossowski, twenty-three, a Rochester, New York, machinist, decided "to do something" after seeing a newsreel showing Madrid being bombed. Decades later he said:

> It took me a lifetime to find out why I went to Spain. The more I read about it, the more I realize it was an instinctive act on my part. It was something that had to be done. Things were so black and white then, with no gray area like we have today. We knew what we were fighting for.

In Pennsylvania, radicals Steve Nelson in Wilkes-Barre, Joe Dougher in Scranton, and John Parks, a transplanted Bluegrass mountain farmer, organized jobless anthracite-coal miners. Dougher had been a miner at twelve, and his organizing activity got him blacklisted by the union and the bosses. Nelson became a laborer in Yugoslavia at twelve, arrived in the U.S. at seventeen, and soon became an organizer of the jobless and a Communist. He rarely had food money and had to plan which families to visit for meals. Since meetings were held on weekends, state and local police, Nelson wrote, regularly arrested "our core group of organizers Friday night and jailed them until Monday morning." However, the three men were able to enroll fifteen thousand to twenty thousand people in three years.

The three led a hunger march of about five thousand jobless to Harrisburg, only to be halted at the city limits by heavily armed, motorized state police. The radicals found farm families willing to house them in barns for the night. In the morning the trucks rolled into Harrisburg and the marchers finally won lodging at the state fairgrounds.

At the capitol they asked the legislature to hear four speakers, one white, one black, one from Pittsburgh, and one from Philadelphia. They were granted a single speaker and confined to the galleries. But as their man rose to speak, three others, reported Nelson, "tied ropes to gallery banisters, slid down, and mounted the podium." Young protestors slid down the ropes and took aisle seats near their representative. Dougher, Parks, and Nelson decided to volunteer for Spain.

Despite their youth and lack of military experience, the American volunteers shared an intense interest in reading about the current issues, past events, novels, and poetry. Many admitted: "We often read in libraries or borrowed books."

Recruitment of volunteers was largely in the hands of the U.S. Communist party, but many others, such as doctors and military experts, had key roles in passing on people's fitness. Selection committees eliminated married men and those with dependents, and insisted on keeping a balance between Communist party members and others. Herbert Matthews of the *New York Times* visited the Americans in their trenches at Madrid and filed this report:

> You cannot dismiss these youngsters with the contemptuous label of "Reds." They are not fighting for Moscow, but for their ideals and because they would rather die than see a Fascist regime under any shape or auspices installed in the United States. The American battalions are unique in one respect, among all the Internationals: They remain American to the core. . . . None of the Internationals are so conscious of their nationality.

Sam Walters, at nineteen, left a WPA job to volunteer for Spain, "caught up in the fervor of youth." He brought a love of books to the trenches at Jarama.

Though American to the core, they were highly unusual volunteers. Seventy were women, and two gained official combat status. In an age of lynch law and discrimination, upwards of eighty were African Americans. Ernest Hemingway met many of them and estimated that half were Communists, or members of the Young Communist League. This oddly mixed, idealistic band was ready to shoulder arms against fascism's best trained and mechanized armies.

For the first time a host of women journalists, many from the battlefield, brought Spain's titanic struggle for liberty to the U.S. public. These included Dorothy Parker, Edna Vincent Millay, Lillian Hellman, Simone Weill, Dorthy Thompson, Emma Goldman, Josephine Hebst and Martha Gellhorn.

27

FOUR

Training Americans

O n December 17, 1936, Hermann Goering summoned a group of elite industrialists and officials for the first announcement of a world war. Goering's words for this momentous occasion were measured and dramatic: "We live in a time when the final battle is in sight. We are already at the threshold of mobilization and we are already at war. All that is lacking is the actual shooting."

Joe Whelan, Robert Raven, and the other ninety-four Americans who boarded a passenger liner, the *Normandie,* on Christmas Day en route to Spain had no inkling of this secret meeting. But they were convinced that fascism in

Sailing in early 1937 on the *Ile de France* as "tourists" are U.S. volunteers, including Irving Goff *(second from left)*, Harry Hakim *(barefoot, next to Goff)*, and Julie Deutch *(bottom, second from left).*

Spain threatened even the United States. The men had purchased uniforms, boots, and winter jackets in army-navy stores. In their cabins they spent hours poring over army training manuals. Recalled Whelan:

> Three of us were crowded into a tiny cabin at the bottom of the ship, and Robert Raven drove us nuts when he insisted on practicing his close-order drill in the room. At first we stayed away from the other volunteers on board, though it was obvious to everyone we were hardly American tourists. Thinking we might have to march off the ship and into battle, we showed up on deck one day in our boots to practice marching.

French border guards waved them through to Spain with a clenched-fist Popular Front salute. But by the time Joe Dallet, at twenty-four a wealthy New Englander and Dartmouth graduate, and the other twenty-five in his group reached Le Havre, the French had sealed the border. Entering Spain was illegal and dangerous. They were warned of pro-Fascist street gangs. The twenty-six were jailed for trying to reach Spain, but a Popular Front lawyer won their release.

Perilous crossings over the Pyrenees often took place at night, with no lights and at a rapid pace with little rest. Sometimes men collapsed and had to be carried through deep snowdrifts. At times winds blew so strongly that men hugged the frozen ground. Harry Hakim described one morning arrival:

> Everything seemed beautiful. . . . We approached a huge white house from which the Catalonian border patrol rushed out to meet us. Walking to the house, we began to sing. The sun rose in all its glory.

Weary volunteers next went through induction. As they discarded civilian clothes, they

Americans learned how to handle grenades and other aspects of battle, not during training but in the field.

were handed outfits from a dozen armies. Recruit Alvah Bessie described the strange scene:

> Everywhere you looked you could find material for laughter: enormous men trying to shoehorn themselves into tiny garments, thin men in colossal trousers that could be wrapped around their waists, tall men with short pants and short men with coats that would fit a giant. The caps, coats, jackets, overcoats, and ponchos were gray, green, olive drab, khaki, in all manner of styles; no two looked alike. They were apparently the hand-me-downs of a dozen different armies. . . . Men were wandering in a bewildered fashion through the room and the courtyard, trying to find someone who had clothes that would fit them, offering to swap.

Basic training was very short and did little to prepare men for battle. Working rifles, live am-

29

American machine gunners learn on the job.

children. Some set up instruction in reading and writing. Recalled Harry Hakim:

> The kids were neglected or orphaned, and they were a welcome diversion. You know how alive kids are! We had classes at least two or three times a week, two hours a day during lunchtime, and would call all the kids around, those twelve and up who worked for us. Only some of the kids could read, those from Madrid. We met in the barracks, dining room, or any room. You would take a kid's hand for hours and show him how to write his name-a totally new experience, and finally he would get to where he could write a very simple letter home. A lot of kids wrote home for the first time in their life. They would get a letter from back home, saying, "My mother can't understand where did I learn to read." (They answered:) "Americano, Lincolns taught me how to read."

Joe Whelan plays jacks with Spanish children.

munition, and skilled instructors were busy at the front. "We were handed Czarist rifles made by Remington and fired three shots into a hill," Charles Nusser reported. "That was combat training." After long hikes and drills with sticks, men were assembled and sent off to war. More than a few died on their first day, peering over the top of trenches, or within a week, victims of inexperience.

Officer training in the beginning proved hardly more efficient. Leonard Lamb reported "meaningless classes conducted in seven languages, and English was not one of them." Most officers were chosen after battle conditions proved their leadership.

At their Tarazona base and elsewhere, many Americans took a special interest in the Spanish

A strong commitment to defending democracy in Spain kept morale high. Psychiatrist William Pike, thirty-four, served on a U.S. screening committee that informed idealistic young men "to expect cold meals, physical hardships, and deadly dangers." Then, when he became the first U.S. doctor in Spain, he discovered that a firm belief in their cause kept the troops going, "particularly in battle, alongside comrades to the right and left of them—when they were able to stay together—who shared their values and commitment." At one point Dr. Pike was able to take twenty-eight shell-shocked men hiding in a wine cellar and persuade them to turn a peasant's path into "Pike's Turnpike"-a road for ambulances.

Many of the shell-shocked did go back to soldiering; others joined Dr. Pike's medical unit. Four out of five in Spain who suffered from shell shock returned to units. (During World War II, Major Pike, U.S. Ninth Army, at a "combat exhaustion center" in Germany, found that "about 10 percent of cases returned to duty.") Dr. Pike believed problems and desertions remained low because "our people understood the reasons for fighting, even for their lack of weapons—they knew why things were happening."

Another reason morale was kept high was

Commissar Ralph Bates speaks to tired soldiers.

An International soldier writes home.

Spain's use of the "commissar," a rank unknown in regular armies. It originally developed in nineteenth-century citizens' armies, which lacked regular military officers. Most of Spain's career military officers had joined the rebels, so on company, battalion, brigade, and division levels, republican army commanders had to share responsibility and power with commissars. The idea was based on a belief that a citizens' army will fight harder if it is informed. Commissars tried to make life easier and patiently explained the military and political decisions that sent men over the top.

Commissars could make what they wanted of the job. Ralph Bates was asked by men at Jarama to act as bard, or public storyteller: "With a bare synopsis jotted down on the back of an envelope, I used to improvise novellas and stories as a means of giving instruction on Spanish social life."

Some commissars improved morale by sharing tender moments with soldiers, and by securing better food and faster delivery, more frequent showers and city passes, better clothing, more reading material. They were committed to carrying complaints by lowly privates to high authorities.

Some commissars strutted. Marion Noble became a commissar but "never wore the damn stripe because a few made such asses of themselves."

"We called them 'comic-stars,'" recalled Harry Hakim. "Some wore dandy uniforms and wanted to lecture us when we wanted decent food, a good delousing unit, and a shower. It was a democratic army, we talked back, didn't accept everything . . ."

"The first to advance, last to retreat," commissars faced a casualty rate higher than that of infantrymen.

The Lincoln Brigade was an unlikely army. It liked to discuss everything. During a drill a screeching officer upset teacher and poet Leo Grachow. "Is that any way to talk to comrades?" he asked Bob Steck.

A Spanish general said Americans "fight like hell," but were "the most difficult to handle." They hated military life and had trouble with authority. As best they could, they guarded their gentle souls from war's terrible demands. One night on the battlefield Alvah Bessie became worried about the impact on the other soldiers of his happy conversation with a buddy.

We both laughed, but we did not laugh for very long, for it is difficult to laugh at night on a road behind the lines in a country at war; the hills threw back our laughter, and the sentries we passed, standing along by the side of the road, must have felt lonelier for our laughter.

Because of a shortage of guns, International Brigaders often trained using farm implements.

The Lincoln Battalion lines up on May 1, 1937.

Part II

To Fight Fascism

FIVE

Jarama

On February 15, training was halted, and the men, having voted themselves the Abraham Lincoln Battalion, were trucked to a bullring called El Monumental. They were lectured about liberty and then greeted by seven American nurses and the chief surgeon, Dr. Edward Barsky. Captain Robert Merriman, a California economics graduate student, became their first commander, and they were made part of the Fifteenth International Brigade.

The Lincolns took up positions in the Jarama valley south of Madrid, with orders to hold the highway that connected Valencia with Madrid. Captain Merriman saw that each volunteer fired off a few shots from his Imperial Russian rifle. For most it was the first experience with a loaded gun. Finding that their assigned position was a perfect target for artillery and aircraft, the men named it "Suicide Hill." Their first fatality came when Charles Edwards, in a forward trench, told others to keep down and peered over the edge himself. A sniper's bullet crashed into his head.

After earlier advances were repulsed, republican General Gal ordered four hundred untested Lincolns to lead a charge. Section leaders Oliver Law and Walter Garland opened fire with the Machine Gun Company's four 1914 Maxims. A republican tank provided the rest of their cover.

A Spanish battalion moved on their right and

Nurses of the Fifteenth Brigade with an ambulance donated to the Mac-Pap Battalion.

a Slav battalion advanced on their left as the Americans, facing withering enemy machine gun fire, dove for cover or keeled over. "We fired until our rifles burned our hands," one reported. At dark, men crawled back to their lines, and patrols set out to carry back the 127 dead and 225 wounded.

For their bravery, three black Americans were promoted: Oliver Law became Machine Gun Company commander, Walter Garland became lieutenant, and Doug Roach succeeded Law as section leader. On the fifth day, seventy un-

The Lincoln Brigade moving out to fight.

The Jarama machine-gun company included Oliver Law, the only one with military bearing.

Winter lookout over sandbags.

trained new recruits joined them. Some, like Robert Kirby, a New York street kid who, at seventeen, had lied about his age to go to Spain, still wore civilian clothes. They were getting lessons from the ten-day veterans when General Gal again ordered the Lincolns to spearhead a charge on Pingarron Hill.

International Brigade members advancing.

He determined to have his newly arrived troops capture Pingarron Hill "at any cost." He did not know it was impregnable. Without the modern communications of their foes, government forces lacked vital information. Heavy artillery, tanks, and twenty bombers were promised, but only a few cannons and planes appeared.

Caption Merriman called headquarters to insist an attack was suicidal, but he was overruled. At noon Merriman decided he must lead the assault. The Lincoln Battalion members, yelling as they charged, were cut down. When a bullet ripped into Merriman's left shoulder, breaking it in five places, he was pulled back.

Until then no one knew that three lines of interlacing machine-gun fire protected Pingarron. John Tisa said: "Cross fire from many machine guns made an impenetrable steel wall against the advance. More groups and sections went over." Recruit Kirby sprinted as fast as he could, fell down, got up, and ran again. He remembered his rifle, aimed, pressed the trigger a few times, and it jammed. He did not know how to fix it.

Joe Rehill's diary recorded he "never knew there were so many bullets in the world, and all of them seemed to shoot around me. I see an-

Wall newspapers become a favorite means of communication for the International Brigade at Jarama.

other comrade who came across with me on the S.S. *Paris.* His gun was jammed, poor guy was actually crying. I can understand how he feels; like myself, he never saw a rifle before."

Rains drenched men and ruined rifles. The last five hundred yards was a dash up a thirty-degree incline in the open, but some made it. While Spaniards, Slavs, and British, realizing it was hopeless, withdrew, the Lincolns continued forward.

Nurse Lini Fuhr had been among those who smiled and waved when the Lincolns left the bullring for the front. Now she saw them at her field hospital:

> Within four hours after the battle had begun we had ninety-three wounded. Our hospital was equipped for five-hundred. A little later, the same day, we had two-hundred. I was on the first floor when they came in. Those who had died en route to us were left in the bitter-cold courtyard. Occasionally from among the dead we heard a moan and found life.
>
> The wounded lay on the floor, and two or

three lay on each bed. First we fought to keep them alive. Later we got their names, in order to list them as wounded. When we had time, we went through clothing matted with blood on cold, stiff dead men to see if they had letters on them or any identifying information. I cut through clothing of boys I had danced with on the way to Spain. My eyes were heavy with lack of sleep and unshed tears. There was no time to cry. The crying would have to come later.

Nurse Frederika Martin wrote home about treating . . .

> . . . bullets in the flesh and bones of the best youth of the world. . . . There is nothing impersonal about it. Those patients are our comrades, are part of us. When they suffer we suffer. There is a terrific emotional drain always.

By the end of the day only 67 of the 450 Lincolns had escaped the bullets and shells. All of the battalion's officers were wounded or killed. Reporter Ernest Hemingway called it an "idiotic" attack, "an act of monumental stupidity," and some veterans agreed with his comment" . . . it was a tragic, criminal mistake."

The gruesome results also created the first Lincoln deserters, including young Kirby, untouched by bullets but seared by the massacre. He spent the night with two other shaken Americans in nearby hills. The next day they returned to camp and were allowed to rejoin the ranks without questions. A volunteer army needs ways to forgive.

The Lincoln Battalion's daring at Jarama kept open the highway that linked Madrid and Valencia. The battle was neither victory nor defeat, but a holding action that cost too many lives. The Americans' courage demonstrated an ability to work as shock troops, and Spanish generals would call on them for this again and again.

Following the bloodbath, the Lincolns dug in at Jarama, where the fighting lulled to a stalemate that swung between deadly boredom and sudden death. The rains came, and men awoke each morning soaked, impatient for a "sunny Spain."

Poet Edwin Rolfe, who edited the battalion journal, *Volunteer for Liberty*, wrote of the arrival of their most famous supporter, Ernest Hemingway. The famous author's presence instilled in men "some of his own strength and quiet unostentatious courage."

Soldiers amused themselves with wall newspapers at Jarama—featuring news from home, men's stories, poems, cartoons, and impressions of the war. Begun as a diversion, the newspapers soon served as cultural exchange and emotional release.

By May, enough new recruits had arrived in Spain to form a second unit, the George Washington Battalion. Later infusions of soldiers, particularly Canadians, led to another battalion named Mackenzie-Papineau, known as MacPaps, to honor two nineteenth-century heroes of Canada's struggle for independence.

Maury Colow, eighteen but looking younger, was appointed a section commander. He resigned in favor of Hugh Bonar, a Scot, saying: "The men felt better that way. Bonar at least shaved."

Tired, disgusted survivors of Pingarron Hill rested, exercised, and had a lot of time to think about their dear friends lost. Morale soon became a serious problem.

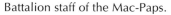

Battalion staff of the Mac-Paps.

Mobile shower units were very popular with the Americans.

Soldiers' monument at Jarama: TO OUR FALLEN COMRADES—OUR VICTORY IS YOUR VENGEANCE, June 1937.

Brunete

To "handle" the grumbling in the Lincoln Battalion after Jarama, Steve Nelson arrived in Spain. Nelson combined the steel will and gritty courage of a Depression organizer with a warm appreciation for human frailties. His smile outlasted battles, and his "Hiya, old-timer" made raw recruits feel wanted. Nelson related easily to working men and women, college professors, and those who disagreed with his radical views.

One of the first sights that greeted him was a group of Lincolns, convicted of such minor crimes as being late after leave, being forced to dig a ditch under armed guards. "They're volunteers," he protested, and won not only their release but a new approach to discipline. His efforts and concern soon had men going into battle, muttering prayerfully, "Don't let them get Steve."

When Lincoln Commander Marty Hourihan was promoted to the Fifteenth Brigade staff, Steve Nelson was on the committee that selected Oliver Law as the new commander. A

During a lull in battle at Brunete, Lincoln Battalion volunteers pose for a photograph. *(Rear, left to right)* unknown, Eli Bregelmor, Harry Hakim, Dennis Jordan, Spaniard, Harry Fisher, Steve Nelson, unknown. *(Front, left to right)* Sol Zalon, Doug Roach, unknown, unknown.

Commander Oliver Law became the first Afro-American in history to lead an integrated U.S. army. He died at Brunete, leading his men into battle.

man who had served six years in the segregated U.S. Army's Twenty-fourth Infantry and could not rise above the rank of sergeant because he was black now led the Americans in Spain. Nelson recalled Law as six foot two and powerfully built,

> . . . more serious than jovial, but never harsh; he was well liked by his men. . . . When soldiers were asked who might become an officer—ours was a very democratic army—his name always came up. It was spoken of him that he was calm under fire, dignified, respectful of his men, and always given to thoughtful consideration of initiatives and military missions.

"Because he had the most experience and was best suited for the job," said Nelson, he was made commander. Not until the Korean War did the U.S. Army break this racial barrier.

The battles at Jarama had saved the Madrid-Valencia road, but Madrid remained surrounded by rebels on three sides. To prepare to launch its first offensive to push back the rebels, Spain began to shape a regular army, with a unified command, out of its voluntary citizen militias—a bricklayers' section here, a bakers' union unit there.

By March, when an Italian army at Guadalajara attempted to complete the encirclement of Madrid, it was defeated with the help of "the Garibaldis," the Italians in the International Brigade. Mussolini had denied his army was in Spain, but now three hundred captured Italian troops and officers proved that they were.

As the Madrid front quieted down, rebel forces turned their attention to the Basque region in the north. There, Spain's Catholics were fervent in their religion and in support of the republic. On April 26, 1937, Nazi Condor Legion bombers, in Europe's first terror bombing, pulverized the picturesque holy city of Guernica.

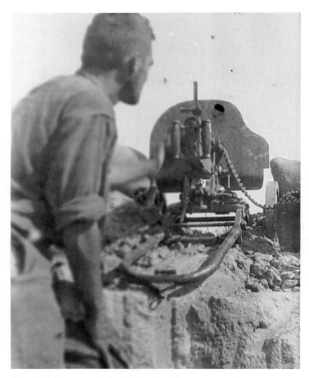

Sam Walters manning his machine gun at Brunete.

A world witnessed fascism's total war on civilians.

By July, Spain was ready to launch its first offensive. It aimed to relieve pressure on Madrid and to divert the rebels attacking the Basques. Led by Law and Nelson, the Lincolns marched to Brunete, just west of Madrid. They paused for a large Fourth of July dinner, then hurried on. As they neared the front at Brunete, Nelson saw the first results of battle:

> . . . stretcher-bears with the first wounded—the blood seeping through the canvas strikes a chill. You wonder who the man is. Is he hit bad? Are many getting it? Will we be successful?

In July's heat, the Lincolns and the newly arrived Washington Battalion, sweating and out of water, crawled to within four hundred yards of the town of Villa Nueva de la Canada. They had the support of Soviet tanks, but bullets sprayed them, reported Harold Smith, like "sudden, vicious squalls." Men had hardly scratched a trench out of hard, dusty earth when they were ordered to attack. By evening they had captured the town but had run out of supplies and food. The rebels rushed in thirty-one battalions, and nine batteries of artillery and its Condor Legion swept the skies.

Medical services used mules to carry the wounded to ambulances. Dr. Irving Busch, chief U.S. surgeon, found "the number of wounded pouring in was so great that numerous surgical teams were kept busy with practically no time for sleep." But the next target, Mosquito Ridge, had to be charged. Harry Fisher wrote:

> I was thirsty, scared, shaky. I looked at the other comrades. Some were fingering their bayonets, others looking over their rifles, some were smiling as though they were going on a picnic, others were expressionless. Then Commander Law's voice booms out: "Let's go, comrades." With bayonets facing forward, our fingers on the triggers, over we went. Just as soon as we got to the top of the hill, their machine guns and rifles opened up. What deadly music that was. But on we went.

Another major assault by the fifteen hundred men of the Fifteenth Brigade was announced for 10:00 A.M. on July 9 by Commander Law. Mosquito Ridge still had to be taken from rebels in fortified positions. Law jumped into the lead, Fisher recalled, "running to the top of the hill" waving his men on. He did not "attempt to protect himself and in a matter of seconds, machine-gun fire ripped into him." His friend Jerry Weinberg crawled out and pulled him to the rear. "He died less than an hour later," Fisher recalled. Nelson was temporarily in command.

A rebel counterattack began with Nazi Heinkel planes outnumbering government

Harry Fisher *(right)*

planes twenty to one.

The two American battalions lost half their men and merged to become the Lincoln-Washington Battalion. (The full name never stuck.) Among the dead was the beloved battalion chef, Jack Shirai, a longshoreman and Japanese citizen from California. Wanting to fight rather than cook, Shirai finally grabbed the rifle he kept in his kitchen and headed for the front line and a machine-gun crew. Captain Walter Garland, twice wounded at Jarama, was again wounded in the knee when he crawled over an exposed hill to save the mortally wounded Leo Kaufman.

On July 18, Franco's forces launched an offensive that could not be contained, and Fifteenth Brigade units retreated. The United Press reported "a bombardment, the heaviest, perhaps, that any troops have ever experienced." Exhausted men sought rest and sleep. Harold Smith found that men "could stand in their sleep. One guy would stop and the rest would domino

Jerry Weinberg *(left)* and Oliver Law at Jarama on June 8, 1937. Weinberg, in New York, and Law, in Chicago, helped evicted families move back into their homes. In Spain they became the best of friends. Weinberg crawled through enemy fire to carry back his mortally wounded friend at Brunete on July 9, 1937.

Japanese volunteer and beloved cook, Jack Shirai, meets reporter Bob Minor *(left)*.

against him. The officers would have to kick the men awake." Smith awoke once "to find I had been sleeping in a kneeling position."

The Lincoln-Washington Battalion and other Internationals were ordered back into battle. Men grumbled and talked of desertion but headed toward the front. Then a motorcyclist brought the news that they could continue the withdrawal. A handful of Lincolns and other Internationals had begun to talk of mutiny.

In a few days Brunete fell to enemy hands, and the stalemate near Madrid returned. The Lincolns and other republican forces had fought gallantly, and it took a huge diversion of rebel power from the Basque front to defeat them. The government lacked the planes, tanks, and firepower of their foes. That was to become increasingly clear and increasingly crucial.

The burial of Jack Shirai during a battle.

Aragon

By August, new recruits and men who had returned from hospitals had rebuilt Lincoln Battalion strength to five hundred. They relaxed behind the front near Madrid, played baseball, and entertained the eager children who trooped after them. Armed with two-day passes, many enjoyed visits to a Madrid that remained the center of Spain's resistance. Of this "marvelous city," *New York Times'* Herbert Matthews wrote:

> Here is the hub of the universe. Here is where one finds the indomitable will to fight this war out to the bitter end. Here is courage, idealism, patience and fortitude . . .

The Hotel Florida became a meeting place for Lincolns on leave. The hotel served only garbanzo beans, but a friendly Ernest Hemingway invited Lincolns to share his foreign delicacies and liquor.

As the Americans prepared under Commander Hans Amlie, orders to move out came so suddenly that Edwin Rolfe and David White had to bang on Madrid hotel doors before dawn, searching for sleeping Lincolns. They rousted 192 men, and by ten in the morning they were handed bread and canned fish and piled into trucks for the front. The Lincolns were launched into a new offensive.

The aim was to capture Saragossa, east of Madrid in the Ebro valley, to break a rebel ring

Lincoln Battalion men join a circle dance with Spanish women as many watch.

encircling the Basque armies there and to lift the pressure on Madrid. As dawn broke on August 24, Charles Nusser, at twenty-one a veteran of Jarama and Brunete, wearing a sleeveless white shirt, led the first company. "He dropped our anxiety down to zero," remembered Herman Rosenstein, a twenty-two-year-old bookkeeper. There was strong tank support, and by the next day Lincolns charged into Quinto and their first hand-to-hand combat.

U.S. engineers repair road to Quinto, cut off by rebel forces.

Steve Nelson, pistol in hand, joined a group of five that banged on doors, yelling for citizens to leave. A beam was used to break down the doors when they received no answers. Civilians, nuns, and priests were guided to safety and given coffee.

Finally, only Quinto's church remained in enemy hands. Its rebel machine guns sprayed the ground for two hundred yards, so it had to be assaulted by cannons and then charged. Nusser estimated that soon two hundred rebel troops surrendered, some yelling "Viva Rusia! Viva Rusia." He told them "that we were Americans and Spainiards, and that there were no Russians here. It was quite evident that the Fascists had done an excellent propaganda job," and the rebel troops believed they were fighting Communists. Lincolns, with minor losses, were jubilant about their part in Quinto's capture and the taking of a thousand prisoners.

Ruins of Belchite were left by Franco as a reminder of "the destruction of the 'Reds.'" Actually, Belchite was pounded into rubble by his Nazi and Fascist planes.

48

Before they had time to savor the victory, the Lincoln's marched twenty miles to Belchite, again to be used as shock troops against a force three times their number. Commander Amlie was wounded and replaced by Leonard Lamb. Three company commanders were hit by snipers in the first fifteen minutes. Republican antitank guns lobbed six shells at snipers hiding in a church.

Manny Lancer, machine-gun commander, was in the assault on the church's three entrances. They had to be rushed simultaneously. "There was a quick, short, bloody battle of hand grenades and bayonets, and the Americans were masters of the church."

The battalion advanced to new barricades down the street and suddenly faced rebel officers. Some, throwing hand grenades, made their escape. That night, Commissar Dave Doran, who replaced a wounded Steve Nelson, brought up a sound truck. He hoped that what fire and shell could not do, propaganda might. Loudspeakers played the Spanish national anthem and blared a speech in Spanish, written by Doran, calling for surrender.

Within an hour a young officer who spoke English crossed the barricade to negotiate with Chief of Staff Merriman, Captain Lamb, and Doran. They tried to convince him his rebels were surrounded by vast firepower. An excited Lincoln messenger came up to announce: "Captain, a division of tanks has just arrived." A startled Lamb answered, "Good, get them into the orchards." Soon another runner interrupted to report: "Captain Lamb, some light artillery has just arrived." Showing less surprise, Lamb said, "Good, have them ready to move up." The young rebel officer returned to his men with what he had seen and heard, and by morning two hundred rebels surrendered.

Isolated enemy pockets held out with the ferocious tenacity that has been the hallmark of

The Lincoln Battalion on the road from Belchite.

49

A pensive Edwin Rolfe, who served as editor of *Volunteer for Liberty.*

civil wars. The Lincolns charged in small groups from one narrow street and tiny house to the next. They stormed basements, fought with bayonets on balconies, and fired at snipers hiding behind windows or on rooftops. A desperate fight for every house and street continued as small U.S. squads spread into the town. One squad was led by seaman Bill Bailey, who politely knocked on doors and asked people to please come out. Then he saw a friend shot as he opened a door. After that Bailey and his men shouted from the street and lobbed grenades into windows when there was no answer.

By September 6, the Lincolns had helped liberate Belchite, which Republican General Rojo had called the Aragon's "most strongly fortified point." Ben Sills was only in his sixth day in Spain. He began trembling and could not stop for two days.

Captured troops, according to Carl Geiser, "most of them kids eighteen and nineteen years old," pointed out two officers who "tried to keep them from surrendering, and [had actually] killed a number who tried to surrender." Two Lincolns executed the two rebel officers. Franco's forces, acting out policy decisions, had slain 200,000 captured civilians and foes. Republican troops, in violation of orders, killed an estimated 10,000 to 20,000. This incident was the only one involving Americans.

The victories in the Aragon earned praise from Spanish General Rojo, who wrote of the

Lincolns' "superiority and passion." Visiting the front, Ernest Hemingway said, "Since I saw them last spring, they have become soldiers." He thought cowards and romantics had departed, and: "Those that were left were tough, with blackened, matter-of-fact faces, and after seven months they knew their trade." *Times* reporter Matthews wrote they were "good fighters who knew they were good . . . and had made the American battalion as famous as the Thaelmann, Garibaldi and Dimitrov battalions."

By then the Americans had earned a place in Spanish hearts. Marion Noble recalls local people "who wouldn't even take pay for doing our laundry-and brought us back the soap we handed them besides-gave us the best seats in restaurants, invited us to their homes to share their tiny pieces of meat, all they had—the only place in the world I met people like that."

Heartened by the victories in the Aragon, Edwin Rolfe, editor of *Volunteer for Liberty,* enthusiastically wrote to his wife: "We know we're going to win. . . . We have a real army now." He was unduly optimistic. Franco regularly received new weaponry from Germany and Italy and oil from the United States. England and France made sure the Spanish republic's border was still closed, and ships of many nations rode the high seas to enforce an embargo against Spain.

Posing with Spanish women and children, Lincoln Brigaders never lost sight of whom they were fighting for.

EIGHT

Behind the Lines

After the victories at Quinto and Belchite, the Lincoln Battalion, said Ernest Hemingway, "fought as well as American fighting men have fought anywhere." Spanish General Jose' Miaja called them "brave, courageous and fine warriors."

Not all U.S. volunteers served in the Lincoln Battalion, though. Spanish-speaking Americans often found their way into Spanish companies. Other Americans joined outfits they admired. Many accepted assignments in medical, mechanical, and guerrilla units.

Recruiters for transport units sometimes waited for volunteers as they came sliding down the Pyrenees. "Coming from the U.S., we were asked about our mechanical skills as soon as we arrived in Spain," said Louis Bortz. He became a driver for the Thaelmann Battalion of Germans. Jim Yates explained why he also volunteered as a driver for them:

> They were the first IB [International Brigade] to fight at Madrid. I admired their courage. They had fought Hitler and his Brown shirts in the streets of German cities. Many had been in Nazi concentration camps. I learned that language is not as big a problem as you might think among good men who fight for a just cause . . . Also they knew some English and we both knew some Spanish.

Albert Chisholm and George Wates, ambulance drivers.

Marion Noble, a detroit auto worker who strummed his Tennessee guitar, was in charge of 150 to 200 "precious vehicles" and "could hardly keep up with all the repair work." Jack Quinones remembered how no one volunteered to be a chauffeur until a French officer assured them "the chances of being blown sky high . . . were most excellent." Many then rushed forward.

Constantly under bombardment, drivers delivered food and supplies to front lines and returned carrying the wounded. They had to out-

52

At Albicete auto-park, Bob Steck *(standing)* speaks to drivers and mechanics.

said, "Well, she had to go because of her husband." I got furious and screamed, "He is there because of me! Not, I want to go because of him!" The chauvinism was just unbelievable, although it was camouflaged at the time, and you had to be very alert to fight it.

Finally I went, I don't know as what, I think a nurse's aide, although it was clear I was going to be a driver. They didn't say driver on my papers. I don't think they said anything, although I was in a group with nurses like Salaria Key . . .

The first of 130 U.S. medical people, led by surgeon Edward Barsky, arrived in Spain weeks after the first Lincolns. Volunteers supposedly had been carefully examined by U.S. committees. But one day psychiatrist William Pike, who had served on a New York examining committee, was surprised by a man in a hospital who

run enemy fire, strafing, and bombing, race through drenching downpours, snow, or scorching heat. The roads looked like the moon's surface. Many times the Fifteenth Brigade's Transport Unit men were ordered into a large city to steal desperately needed trucks and cars.

To win the right to drive a truck and an ambulance in Spain, Evelyn Hutchins warred against traditional U.S. attitudes about women. An artist and nightclub dancer, she arrived in Spain after her brother and her husband:

> All those people at the American Friends of Spanish Democracy just couldn't accept the fact that a woman could be a driver. I started accusing them of chauvinism, one at a time and then collectively. Of course they denied it, but I wasn't getting my shipping order as a driver.
>
> They tried to get me there as a nurse but I did not have a certificate. They tried clerk-typist. Why the hell would anybody want to send a clerk-typist there? These kinds of stupidities kept galling me and I kept arguing and so finally they

"Nurse" Evelyn Hutchins

A wounded soldier is lifted into an ambulance.

rolled up his pants to show wounds—in a wooden leg.

In Spain, said Dr. Pike, "We learned quickly not to mark our hospitals with red crosses, for that only invited Fascist planes." Nurse Hilda Roberts found terrible medical conditions:

> . . . a shortage of food, men were really emaciated, medicine and medical supplies were low, and hospitals were considered very strange. One woman insisted on calling me a man because I worked in a hospital. . . . I had to pick lice off patients before operations. People had no knowledge of medicine, intravenous feeding was scoffed at. One patient being fed through a tube said, "I'll die if you don't feed me."

Dr. Arnold Donowa, the only black doctor in the Lincolns, had a degree from Howard University. He had left Harlem to serve first as a dental surgeon in the front lines and later in a hospital. Dr. Donowa wrote:

We suffered above all from a lack of instruments and supplies needed for adequate jaw surgery. And frequently we had not even enough gauze and bandages to dress the wounds of the men. There was so great a scarcity of these elementary medical supplies that we had to unwind the bandage one man had used, not cut it away as we do in the United States, have it washed and boiled and then rewound again by the women in the hospital so we'd be able to use them again on another patient. Sometimes it was hard to get blood stains entirely out, but we managed to sterilize the old bandages and made them fit for use again.

We did not have a drop of novocaine in the hospital. . . . This as well as many other indispensable drugs were almost unobtainable in Spain in those final days. There were so many items we take for granted back home, which we lacked in Spain. To reduce jaw fractures, for example, we needed a special kind of this very thin stainless steel wire. A pound of it, only a pound, would have relieved the crises at my hospital for a couple of months. But we didn't have it, nor did we have any x-ray film. We had to work by touch to determine the number of fractures.

Some Americans became guerrillas. Lieutenant Irving Goff left a job as an acrobat to go to Spain and found a career as a commander behind enemy lines. With Lieutenant William Aalto and Alex Kunslich, Goff volunteered for the Fourteenth Army Corps—two thousand men with demolition skills divided into bands operating inside rebel lines in Andalusia and Estremadura.

Goff's band blew up bridges and rail lines, mined roads, and disrupted communications. Not long after, Kunslich was captured and killed. On December 14, 1937, Goff and Aalto, then hardened, experienced guerrillas, were dispatched to blow up a bridge. The unit included two Finns, six Spaniards, and a local guide.

Carrying packs of explosive and tools, the men moved swiftly by moonlight in freezing snow to their target twenty kilometers away. The bridge was unguarded. Cold fingers delicately placed explosives and set timing devices, and Goff's band ran and skidded through the snow to watch the target burst into flames.

Then they set about destroying telephone lines. By this time a cavalry unit galloped after them. The guerrillas fired as they fled, finally eluding pursuers to reach a republican village.

During an offensive on May 23, 1938, Goff and Aalto led a guerrilla assault on Corchuna fortress, which held republican prisoners. In the guise of a relief force, guerrillas entered the fort's guardroom, opened fire, and "…while it lasted it was rough and bloody," said Goff. Once the garrison's officers were shot, soldiers surrendered, and 308 republican prisoners were released. They were handed rifles. Goff's enlarged force then had to break through rebel lines to republican territory. Goff and Aalto brought up

the rear, firing furiously at pursuers, and everyone escaped.

By World War II Goff and his men were among the few Americans with combat experience behind Nazi and Fascist lines.

A Chinese medical team in Spain.

NINE

Teruel

*I*n October 1937, the Lincolns became part of an offensive to capture Saragossa. They and the Canadian battalion fought bravely against a wall of steel, only to be driven back. In December they again launched an assault. This time it was on Teruel, west of Madrid, during a winter of blizzards, the coldest season in memory. Carl Geiser described deadly conditions that included snow three feet deep:

Food froze before it reached the trenches, and anyone who received a very bad wound froze to death before he could be taken to the first aid station.

Lincolns called their outpost the "North Pole."

In January, enemy artillery pounded harder than ever, and in mid-February, Franco swept toward Teruel. But I a snowstorm, Lincolns, led

This section of Teruel was called the "North Pole" in January 1938.

Teruel in January 1938.

by Captain Leonard Lamb, and Canadians counterattacked and captured more than 120 rebels. It was the only night attack Americans made in Spain, and a worried rebel command issued a dispatch that claimed "the Lincoln and Washington brigades have been destroyed."

By February 19, Franco regrouped his forces and marched into Teruel. Huge numbers of troops and hundreds of German and Italian planes provided the edge. At Christmas, when government forces had claimed Teruel, Edwin Rolfe wrote his wife that Teruel could be "the beginning of the end for Franco." A republican offensive had begun with high hopes. But with Franco's air and weapon superiority, it vanished like a tear in the snow.

TEN

The United States Home Front

Jitterbugging to raise funds for the Lincoln Battalion at the Liberty Ball Fiesta, December 10, 1938.

*B*ack in the United States, supporters of the Lincoln Brigade collected signatures on petitions and jitterbugged to raise money for the men overseas. In April 1937, a Friends of the Abraham Lincoln Brigade was formed. Its president was veteran David McKelvy White, Princeton and Columbia graduate, professor of English—his father, a former Ohio governor, was the chairman of the Democratic Party. With branches in major U.S. cities and fifty thousand members, the Friends raided more than $425,000. The Friends supplied medical and financial aid to returning wounded, issued a magazine, *Among Friends,* and sponsored lectures by returning veterans. Trade unions and prominent citizens, such as Henry Luce, publisher of *Life,* and presidential adviser Bernard Baruch, became sponsors. New York headquarters, recalled Al Koslow, sent chocolates, cigarettes, and books to Spain:

> The office was filled with activity. We had more volunteers than we could handle. Packages from all parts of the U.S. addressed to the boys in Spain were routed through our office and sent to Albecete, Spain.

Robert Raven addresses a U.S. audience.

This picket line marched in front of the Italian Embassy in Washington, D.C., on March 23, 1937.

In December 1937, twenty veterans were arrested for picketing a Times Square store that sold Japanese products. In October 1938, others, carrying a Spanish flag, led seven thousand demonstrators into a Chicago German American Bund rally and lustily joined the riot that followed.

Returning veterans spoke at public meetings on the dangers of fascism. Robert Raven, blinded at Jarama, was an impressive speaker, as were Hans Amlie, Walter Garland, and Steve Nelson. Ralph Bates's eloquent voice was heard over the radio and in the major U.S. cities he toured. Friends' meetings were designed to guide public sympathy for Spain into a demand that the U.S. lift the embargo. They were also used by recruiters for the Lincoln Brigade. "Those who want to do more" were handed leaflets with a phone number. The Spanish embassy reported receiving inquiries each week from men who wanted to volunteer. Recruiters claimed that total strangers approached them, pleading to go.

At dances, house parties, and other events, money was raised and people heard about fascism. Doris Schwartz remembered:

> I started going to parties and dances and met men who were not just interested in sports . . . and they talked about Spain. Some went on to volunteer, and many young, beautiful men never returned. This was the beginning of my becoming aware that there was more to life than fun. Soon we were on street corners collecting money in tin cans for Spain, asking people to sign petitions demanding that the embargo be lifted. I learned then and still feel one must give back to society, not just take from it.

Scores of famous reporters and authors brought the distant war to every doorstep and took up the cause of republican Spain. In early 1937, 98 U.S. writers, including Robert Benchley, Erskine Caldwell, John Dewey, Sinclair Lewis, Thornton Wilder, Lewis Mumford, Stephen Vincent Benét, and Upton Sinclair, appealed for help to Spain. A poll by the League of American Writers found that 410 writers favored the republic, one was for Franco, and only 7 were neutral. In Hollywood, writer Ring Lardner, Jr., director John Huston, and actors James Cagney, Humphrey Bogart, Paul Muni, Bette Davis, and others donated money and ambulances to a free Spain. They wished "a speedy victory" to La Pasionaria, the woman who was the "living symbol of the workers' struggle for democracy and freedom." Lardner said "an overwhelming majority of academics and intellectuals of all kinds" supported the republic. Martha Gellhorn, a foreign correspondent and future Mrs. Hemingway, explained the feeling:

> We knew, we just *knew* that Spain was the place to stop fascism. This was it. It was one of those moments in history when there was no doubt.

U.S. public opinion overwhelmingly favored republican Spain. In January 1937, it was by a two-to-one majority, and a year later it rose to three to one. But most citizens supported the embargo and rejected any U.S. involvement in a European war.

The cause of Spanish democracy thrilled artists and intellectuals everywhere. It inspired eloquent words in scribbled letters, diaries, and poems written in trenches. Ralph Bates found:

> . . . times in Spain, moments only as a rule, when my vision of the world was suddenly purified. . . . In those moments, perception put me in touch with a world that was lovely and itself pure. It is hard to describe this sensation but it is the origin of much poetry.

Paul Robeson, world-famous U.S. baritone, sings for the soldiers at University City in January 1938.

This ambulance was sent to Spain. Seated inside is composer W. C. Handy.

On April 4, 1938, three thousand women marched to protest the U.S. embargo on Spain.

John Dos Passos wrote of a Madrid night in the spring:

> From the west came a scattered hollow popping lightly perforating the horizon of quiet. Somewhere not very far away men with every nerve tense were crawling along the dark sides of walls, keeping their heads down in trenches, yanking their arms back to sling a hand grenade at some creeping shadow opposite.

The Franco side was also heard loud and clear through the media. Front-page tales about "Communists" sold more copies than talk about Nazi aggression. The five hundred Soviet officers and technicians in Spain received more media attention than tens of thousands of troops, pilots, and technicians from Italy and Germany. Rebel propaganda exaggerated republican violence against the church. Many U.S. papers adopted Franco's technique of calling republicans "Reds" or "Communists," and the rebels and foreign Fascists "Nationalists."

The battle for the home front was fought almost as hard as the war in Spain, and the stakes were just as high.

Americans increasingly became concerned about U.S. prisoners of Franco. Of 290 Lincolns captured, 176 were shot on the spot. Commissar Carl Geiser was the highest Lincoln Brigade officer to survive capture. He was saved from a firing squad because Italian officers sought Internationals to trade for their prisoners. At the San Pedro de Cardeña concentration camp, he and others resisted as best they could. The prisoners ran the San Pedro Institute of Higher Learning, which offered seventeen classes in sociology and languages, "through geometry, algebra, trigonometry, and calculus. There were classes in radio circuitry, labor history, music and art,"

Geiser wrote. He explained its real purpose:

> No other activity we engaged in was as important as these classes in resisting the dehumanizing and degrading atmosphere of the concentration camp.

Prisoners produced a sparkling Christmas variety show and a regular paper, *The Jaily News*. Their friends and relatives did not forget them. In February 1939, in New York City, a Prisoners' Ball and celebrity auction raised funds. By then, "Relatives of American Prisoners" had collected fifty thousand signatures, asking for their speedy return. In 1939, the last U.S. captives left Spain to homecoming receptions. Geiser became director of the Friends on his return and in 1987 wrote *Prisoners of the Good Fight*. Speaking on his arrival, ex-prisoner Stanley Heinricher told reporters: "We'd do it all over again if we had to."

ELEVEN

Retreat and Flight

*I*n March 1938, Franco forces prepared to launch a full-scale blitzkrieg with planes, tanks, and air power. The five hundred Lincolns in Belchite suddenly faced rebel troops, tanks, and planes along an entire front. For hours the Lincolns held their ground, then fled. Frightened men ran without looking back. Harold Smith stared at twenty advancing tanks:

A wounded Lincoln is helped to the rear.

They open fire. Lincolns fall back from the ridge, carrying wounded, seeking cover, firing, and retreating. We retreat across plains to olive groves and trees, under constant fire of tanks.

Lieutenant Frank Bonetti, badly wounded, was calm. "The curiosity to see how the day would end became stronger than the will to die."

Republican soldiers regrouped and marched as exhausted, foot-sore troops. Retreating men shed clothes, food, packs, canteens, and blanket rolls, and some threw away rifles. Those who paused to make a stand learned the enemy had passed them. The foe waited for their tanks, planes, and artillery to reload and then sped ahead in Ford trucks, ready for the next battle. Soon soldiers and refugees clogged roads. No unit remained intact.

Planes strafed 200 Americans who fled from the roads to the olive fields and finally reached Caspé. Commissar Dave Doran grimly said holding it would allow the army to retreat in order, and for three days 700 men held Caspé. The last night, 250 charged rebels in the hills. Lawrence Cane, who led a squad, said: "Some of us, I believe, were actually unarmed. All we could really do was throw rocks and yell at them." Yet hills were captured and prisoners taken. Lincolns, last to leave Belchite, were the last to evacuate Caspé. General Rojo said their

Commissar Dave Doran *(left)*, Captain Robert Merriman and his wife.

stand provided valuable time.

The enemy finally stopped, and the Lincolns were joined by one hundred perky recruits fresh from Tarazona training. Recruit Alvah Bessie carried books, writing paper, and thread. The men he thought of as heroes were "filthy and lousy; they stank; their clothes were in rags." Men believed dead staggered in, and everyone began to laugh and cry. It was, said one, "a gathering of ghosts."

Battalion strength rose to four hundred again. An art student from Coney Island, New York, Milton Wolff, twenty-two, whose training began as a private only months before, became commander. "He was about the coolest guy I ever met," said Herman Rosenstein. "Nothing shook him."

On March 30, with new Czech and Soviet rifles, machine guns, and grenades, the Lincolns marched through Gandesa. They had no idea that the 80,000 republicans they joined were facing 200,000 rebels who had broken through the front. During the headlong retreat that followed, men fell behind enemy lines. Bessie's company was one of several that stumbled into enemy camps and paid for the error with heavy casualties. The enemy was also confused. Rebel Commander Valino, lacking communication and transportation, asked, "Who actually are the prisoners? We or they?"

Bessie described the fleeing Americans:

> They said the Fascists were on the way, but we didn't care. They said the tanks were coming up, but no one paid any attention. There was no command, there was no authority, there was not even a point to which you could report.

According to Commander Wolff, "There wasn't a man who made the trip who didn't feel death walking by his side." Near Corbera, commanders Merriman and Doran, trapped behind rebel lines, vanished. The Lincolns and Canadians had become shabby, homeless men in search of the Ebro River. Hopelessly lost, some began to follow enemy soldiers who were also headed toward the Ebro. One rifle, twenty bullets, and courage helped Harry Fisher and his buddies follow the rear of a rebel column for two hours. Marty Sullivan whispered to Fisher he was so hungry he hoped the rebels would "stop and dish out some food." Some, like Captain Lamb, "read the North Star" and "headed for the river."

Spring had swollen the Ebro's icy currents, and it was two hundred yards across. Its bridges had been dynamited. Commissar Kenneth Shaker was captured, but he escaped, fled to, and finally swam the Ebro. Commissar Keller and a Canadian were taken prisoner, but Keller punched his captor in the jaw while the Canadian seized his rifle and clubbed him. They swam the Ebro. Others were captured as they sprawled exhausted at the bank. Many died in its swift currents.

On the safe side, Bessie saw Harry Hakim handing out letters:

He read hundreds of names, but only about fifteen men claimed letters. It took him half an hour to read all the names on the letters, and after the first few times nobody would say, "Dead"or "Missing"; we just kept silent.

The last one to swim the Ebro was Captain Milton Wolff:

I don't know how the hell I survived. Olives fell off trees, fruit. A couple of peasants stopped and gave me a piece of bread, some wine. One told me, "Can't swim across river," but I was from Coney Island. When I asked him where were the Fascists, he said, "On both sides." So I dove into the river and I swam around and came out on the same side I went in—not knowing our forces were on the other side. I hid in a hollow of a tree and the Fascists were patrolling...I had to stay there all day and at nightfall I swam across.

By April 15, Franco's forces had cut Spain in two. Only one hundred Americans were left in the Lincoln Battalion.

Red Drummond, Mike Pappas, and Luchell McDaniels at Gandesa. McDaniels, one of more than one hundred Afro-Americans in Spain, was "El Fantastico" because his pitching arm could throw grenades with deadly accuracy.

TWELVE

Farewell

In the summer of 1938, three thousand International volunteers remained in the trenches. The Spanish government considered them among its best troops. They were valuable for other reasons, too. First, their reputation attracted new recruits to the Spanish cause, and second, they carried the hope that England and France might still save Spain.

Less than 450 American volunteers remained in Spain. Three-fourths of the Lincoln Battalion now were young Spanish peasants, fresh from the countryside. "We will be their comrades, their brothers, their teachers and their friends," explained Commissar George Watt. But American spirits sagged, drinking increased, and soon everyone wanted a battle. Among the last thirty Lincolns to join were eight veterans who returned from medical treatment in the U.S. The last to volunteer was Jim Lardner, son of author Ring Lardner. He crossed into Spain as a newspaper reporter with Ernest Hemingway, then decided to enlist.

To relieve rebel pressure on Valencia, the republic launched a surprise offensive. Captain Wolff, now called "El Lobo" by the enemy, announced "the entire Army of the East will participate...over eighty thousand men will be crossing simultaneously." On the moonless evening of July 25, hundreds of boats silently rowed across the Ebro. Lieutenant Aaron Lopoff

The Lincoln Battalion building the Fifteenth Brigade headquarters in August 1938.

said to fellow Brooklynite Alvah Bessie, "It's Prospect Park in the summertime. It's wonderful." At sunrise, as enemy bombs began to fall, the Lincolns' turn came to climb into boats.

The surprise worked and Lincolns captured Fatarella. Marching toward Gandesa, peasants told Bessie how U.S. prisoners . . .

Crossing the Ebro by boat.

. . . had been taken out every night in batches of three to five and shot down. They showed us their unmarked graves and told us (since many of them had been forced to witness these executions as an example) how our men lifted their fists in the Republican salute and shouted, "Death to fascism!"

The enemy continued to reel backward, and the Lincolns overran trenches and captured two hundred men. But Franco's fresh units soon outnumbered republicans three to one, and his superiority in machine guns, artillery, and air power paid off again. Lincolns charged forward only to be driven back by raking machine-gun fire. Many of the raw young native Spanish Lincolns were afraid to charge, often leaving the battle-hardened Americans to move forward without their support.

Finally, less than on hundred Americans were still able to fire a rifle. Hill 666, which Bill Bailey called "the stupidest piece of real estate," was the key to commanding twenty miles of elevation. He recalled:

But there was no way you could dig in, no dirt, all solid rock, so shrapnel fragments splattered in every direction-and you had no way to hide.

68

Fifteenth International Brigade in action at Sierra Pandols, August 1938.

Artillery pounded Lincolns for an unrelenting seven and a half hours. Bessie hugged hard ground and focused on tiny details:

A fly is attracted to your bloody hands and clothes; you shake it off. A louse is crawling in your groin. . . . Dry lips, rising gorge, sweat, and shaking limbs. You look at your hands, filthy and covered with the blood of two men who have finally been taken. You lie and instantly cover your face with your leather jacket when you hear them coming, as though it offered any protection. You throw it angrily from you, knowing yourself a fool, but grasp it instinctively when the whistling is growing louder and your mind tells you this one will be close.

The explosions ended, but men shook through the night. At Hill 666, Lincolns won a citation for "tenacious resistance." The government offensive captured three thousand prisoners and liberated dozens of towns. It would take months for Franco to regain the lost ground. An exuberant Bessie believed these victories not only strengthened the republic but "definitely helped check Hitler-Mussolini aggression elsewhere."

He was unduly optimistic. The democracies, far from Hill 666, were not committed to resist. Nazi troops had seized Austria at dawn on March

Dressing a wound at the front was common.

Led by their officers *(left to right),* Captain Donald Thayer, Major Milton Wolff, and Commissar George Watt, the Lincolns march in Catalonia in October 1938.

12 and made it a military state, and a month later Hitler triumphantly entered Vienna. English and French diplomats began preparing a Munich conference with Hitler and Mussolini. There they decided the future of Czechoslovakia, but that country was not invited, and neither was its main ally, the Soviet Union.

On September 21, Spain's prime minister, Juan Negrin, announced before the League of Nations he was unilaterally withdrawing all International volunteers. He hoped that would focus world attention on a Spain fighting alone against Fascist aggression. He soon regretted his move. It failed to budge Franco, Hitler, or Mussolini and released his best troops when they were still desperately needed.

On September 29, the Munich conference began. France and England gave in to Hitler's demands, and this ended any hope that Spain would be saved or Hitler stopped. Six months later Mussolini invaded Albania, and Hitler controlled Czechoslovakia.

On October 4, the International Brigades were withdrawn. Only the night before, Jim Lardner had been killed. After many fiestas, on October 29 the two thousand surviving Internationals paraded for the last time in Barcelona. Hundreds of thousands packed the line of march, stood on balconies and benches, and hung from trees. Government planes flew overhead.

Led by Major Wolff, who was flanked by his staff officers, two hundred Americans received the loudest cheers and walked through what Wolff called "flowers up to our ankles." Maury Colow said, "The women and children were jumping into our arms, kissing us, calling us sons, brothers, calling 'come back,' weeping. It was a farewell that was indescribable." Rolfe wrote: "It was the most thrilling sight, we agreed, that we had ever seen."

Colow remembered, "It ended in a courtyard where La Pasionaria spoke before these tough Yugoslavs, Germans, American." It was a speech that lived forever in Lincoln memories:

You are history. You are legend. You are the heroic example of democracy's solidarity and universality.

We shall not forget you, and when the olive tree of peace puts forth its leaves again, entwined with the laurels of the Spanish Republic's victory—come back!

La Pasionaria flanked by admiring members of the International Brigade in 1938.

La Pasionaria signs autographs on October 29, 1938, for Major Milton Wolff *(above her)* and other International Brigaders.

"And I never had such an experience," said Colow, "because these men, such tough fighters, every last one of them was crying."

Marion Noble recalled the trip that brought them out of Spain and into France in December 1938.

> The train made an unscheduled stop and I looked down and it is completely surrounded by cops, every three feet, all around. Peasants had gotten on the track and refused to let the train go through. I look out the window and there's hundreds and hundreds of French peasants and they got packages in their arms. They wanted to give us food but French officials are scared half to death there was going to be a revolution.

On January 27, 1939, as the volunteers headed home, President Roosevelt admitted to his cabinet that his embargo had violated old American principles and "had been a grave mistake." Its cost soon became clear.

Returning veterans

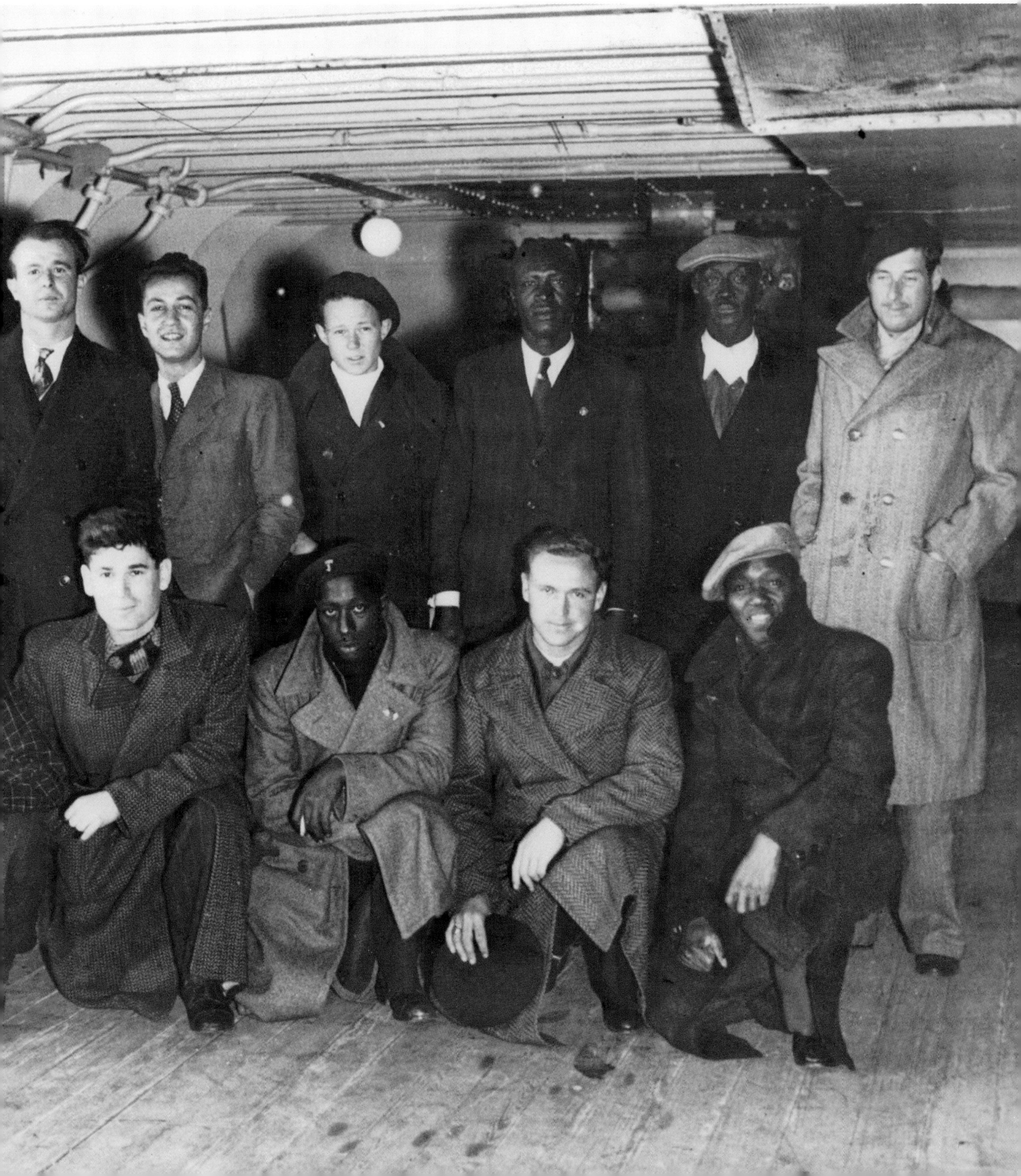

FASCIST SPAIN THREATENS

FASCIST SPAIN

STOP FAS

VETERAN
ABRAHAM LINCO

TO
SH

Anti-Franco demonstration, Madison Square Park, April 1946.

Part III

Bittersweet Homecoming

THIRTEEN

World War II

*H*itler rode into Prague that March 15, 1939, and two weeks later General Franco made himself dictator of Spain. Although he promised reconciliation, Franco began a roundup of republican supporters, which took 200,000 lives and imprisoned another 200,000 (Half a million refugees fled to France, and 7,000, including 5,000 children, accepted exile in the USSR.) Five months after Franco took Spain, a German blitzkrieg rolled into Warsaw and World War II began.

During the war some nine hundred Lincolns served in the U.S. armed forces or its merchant marine. The day Harry Hakim enlisted in the navy, his recruiting officer introduced him to a U.S. bond rally in Miami, Florida: "Harry Hakim fought Hitler and Mussolini in Spain without enough guns and ammunition, and the Fascists drove him out. Harry's with us now! You're not going to let Harry down this time, are you?" After Hakim's stirring speech, citizens bought $100,000 in bonds.

Irving Goff, Bill Aalto, Milt Wolff, and six other Lincolns served in General Bill Donovan's OSS, a U.S. secret service (which became the CIA). Their experience behind German and Italian lines in Spain and their contacts with European underground fighters proved invaluable. In North Africa, Goff's strike force liberated a Nazi concentration camp. Behind German lines in Africa, they gathered information on General Rommel for the British. In Sicily, they slipped twenty-two intelligence teams into southern Italy, and twenty-one of the missions were successful. There Goff made contact with Garibaldis

Lincoln veterans assemble on May Day 1939.

Some 500,000 refugees fled Franco into France, where they were interned.

he had known in Spain who were now leading anti-Nazi partisans. Through Goff, they supplied intelligence services to the Allies.

In Northern Italy, said Goff, "We had eighteen radio teams" with information that Allied headquarters called "the best from any source. . . . We had an overlay map of all the German positions. The American army knew where every German was."

During the war, Lincolns served in every theater of operation. General Evans Carlson sought them out for his famous Carlson's Raiders, and General Joe Stillwell wanted them for his Burma campaigns. For his heroism in the Pacific, Sergeant Hermann Bottcher won a Distinguished Service Cross and battlefield promotion to captain. He was slain on the island of Leyte.

Bill Van Felix, wounded severely on Hill 666 and deferred from the military draft as 4F, joined the merchant marine. Van Felix's ship was in the fleet transporting troops from England to France on D day. Jerry Cook landed in France with the Normandy invasion, and Lieutenant Larry Cane won the French Croix de Guerre at Normandy.

Sergeant Hermann Bottcher

Jerry Weinberg won a Distinguished Flying Cross for bombing raids on the oil refineries at Ploesti, Rumania. Imprisoned in Turkey when his plane came down, he escaped and made his way to British forces in Egypt. He died flying a Liberator over Germany. Infantryman Saul Wellman was wounded in the Battle of the Bulge in Belgium. Infantryman Joe Whelan emerged from that battle to take part in the liberation of the Mauthausen concentration camp. Sergeant Bob Thompson earned the Distinguished Service Cross for heroism in New Guinea.

George Watt was a machine-gunner on a B-17 over Germany. When his plane was downed after its seventh mission, he parachuted into Belgium. Villagers hid him by day and moved him by night through a network "organized, directed, and staffed almost entirely by women." He was supplied with false papers and guided through Brussels, Paris, Bordeaux, across the Pyrenees to Spain, and finally to Gibraltar and the British. Because he was familiar with the anti-Nazi underground, the air force would not risk having him fly over enemy territory. He was made a flight instructor.

Lincoln veterans felt proud that Internationals they knew in Spain were helping to bury fascism. Tito and his partisan commanders tied up twenty-five Nazi divisions in Yugoslavia and eventually liberated their country. Others used their experience in Spain to lead liberation movements behind Nazi lines across Europe and help drive the invaders from their homelands.

During the Cold War era hysteria, Lincoln veterans were tracked by the FBI and the Veter-

Burl Ives and Canada Lee lead a protest march of Lincoln veterans in December 1946.

ans of the Lincoln Brigade [VALB] were labelled members of a "subversive organization" by the Truman administration.

Because Goff, Wolff and Lincolns worked in the OSS, some Congressmen charged "communists had infiltrated our secret service." OSS Director Donovan was told Goff had been on the honor roll of the Young Communist League, and responded, "For the job he did in Africa and Italy, he's on the honor roll of the OSS." After FBI agents visited their employers veterans who were communists, and those who were not, lost their jobs. In World War II Edward A. Carter Jr., an African American Lincoln veteran, was decorated for his heroism but in 1949 he was denied the right to reenlist. In 1997 President Bill Clinton posthumously awarded Carter the Congressional Medal of Honor.

Lincoln veterans entered many a dangerous fight. In 1949 when a Paul Robeson concert in Peekskill was attacked by a white mob, Lincolns helped shield the man who sang for them in Spain. In 1960 in California when HUAC subpoenaed Archie Brown, he defiantly joined the demonstration outside the hearing and refused to testify inside. As police dragged him away, he shouted "Watch this Americanism in action!"

In 1954 the VALB was ordered to register as a "communist organization" under the McCarran Act. Though they faced five years in jail and a $10,000 fine for each day of non-compliance, officers Moe Fishman and Milton Wolff refused to register. In l965 the VALB finally won its appeal to the U.S. Supreme Court.

After Spain, Lincoln veterans resumed their battle to help people of color gain their human rights. As chairman of the Greenwich Village NAACP, James Yates battled school segregation in New York and aided Dr. King's southern crusade. In 1964 when Abe Osheroff worked with African Americans to rebuild a Community Center in Mississippi, his car was dynamited and he

Sgt. Edward Carter went from Spain to World War II and a posthumous Congressional Medal of Honor.

had to carry a .38 and a shotgun. "I had gone abroad, so to speak, to fight in a foreign war," he said. In 1966 Lincoln nurse Ruth Davidow volunteered to provide medical care for African Americans in Mississippi. Three years later she volunteered to serve the medical needs of native Americans who occupied Alcatraz Island, and often was the only white person they allowed on the island.

The VALB was among the first to denounce the Viet Nam war and Maury Colow helped organize "Veterans for Peace." The VALB debunked U.S. interventions in Nicaragua, El Salvador, Grenada and Cuba as "not in the best interests of the American people." Members delivered wheel chairs and 18 ambulances to a Nicaragua under seige by U.S-armed Contras. "As long as you're fighting oppression, for the right of people to determine the way they want to live, Spain is alive," said Abe Smorodin. "After all, Franco was the first Contra." The VALB was among the first U.S. groups to demand freedom for Nelson Mandela.

Aging Lincolns, some in wheel chairs or on crutches, joined marches for civil liberties, and against nuclear weapons, and U.S. militarism abroad. By the 1960s young demonstrators enthusiastically embraced Lincoln veterans as heroes and role models.

The VALB also opposed the U.S. trade embargo against Cuba, and nurse Hilda Roberts helped fill "a yellow school bus" with medical supplies and computers to challenge the embargo. When U.S. officials halted it at the Mexican border, Roberts and others staged a hunger strike until the bus was released. In 2000 VALB members marched to support the Puerto Rican demand that the U.S. Navy leave a Vieques Island it used for a target range.

By 2000, U.S. monuments to the Lincoln Brigade were in place in Seattle, Washington and Madison, Wisconsin. "The Good Fight" and "Forever Activists," two Oscar-nominated movie documentaries, celebrated the veterans' anti-fascist record.

Lincolns reminded the world that in World War II Franco's Blue Division fought alongside Nazi troops on the Russian Front. The VALB sent clothing, sheets, and medicines to Spain's political prisoners. But U.S. presidents, seeking Cold War bases in Spain, sent Franco billions in aid, and in 1956 gained his admission to the UN. After Franco died in 1975 Spain returned to republicanism, and in less than a generation the dictator's popularity sank to 2 percent.

Veterans of the Lincoln Brigade, including Abe Smorodin *(left)*, Len Levinson *(center)*, and Charles Nusser *(right)*, march against apartheid in South Africa in the 1980s.

FOURTEEN

Return in Triumph

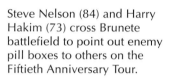

Steve Nelson (84) and Harry Hakim (73) cross Brunete battlefield to point out enemy pill boxes to others on the Fiftieth Anniversary Tour.

*F*or two weeks in October 1986, 120 members of the Abraham Lincoln Brigade and 260 of their widows, relatives, and friends returned to Spain. It was the fiftieth anniversary of a civil war the world has almost forgotten. They came at the invitation of mayors, artists, and labor leaders. Hundreds of Europeans from thirty nations, survivors of other International Brigades, also attended. Many could not attend—about half of the International volunteers lay buried in a coun-

try they boldly defended. Others died in World War II, fighting the same Fascist enemy.

Americans had been the youngest of the volunteers in 1937 and now composed the largest group of all the nationalities present. They arrived in a country that showed few visible signs of the Franco dictatorship that had ruled for thirty-six years. In Madrid's lovely El Retiro Park, where the Fiftieth Anniversary Tour first assembled, men and women in their seventies and eighties peered into lined faces they might have known half a century ago. They shook hands and hugged, and many cried softly. Language was a barrier, but eyes moistened and comrades touched.

The new national government sat out the homage. Perhaps it felt Spain was still too bitterly divided to celebrate these opinionated ex-soldiers of the republic. But local mayors, labor leaders, and cultural figures soon turned a simple tour into a triumph. World TV coverage included two crews from Japan filming anything about native son Jack Shirai of the Lincolns. Three U.S. TV crews jammed the entrance to the first night's banquet so that tables could be reached only by sloshing through a thick stew of wires, cameras, lights, and technicians.

Most ceremonies were run by local mayors, but some moments soared on their own. During the first cultural homage in Madrid's Palacio de Congresós, poets, dancers, and singers offered a dazzling display of Spain's traditions. Songs, poems, and movies of the war were mixed with long-winded speeches. Steve Nelson, commander of the Abraham Lincoln Brigade, won the crowd by confining his remakes to a single American minute. At one point the young Madrid audience spontaneously stood up, held hands,

Young Spaniards in Madred honor veterans by holding hands and singing.

82

Steve Nelson *(left)* and Spanish General Lister are part of a huge Madrid crowd honoring the International Brigade.

swayed, and chanted, "We are paying you homage."

The unplanned climax came when Lincoln vet Ed Balchowsky walked on stage, waving an empty sleeve. "Although I went home with one hand, I gained more than I lost—thanks to the Spanish people," he said as people began to cry. Forced to abandon a life as a concert pianist, but having learned to sketch rebel machine-gun emplacements, he returned home to career as an artist. Still a masterful one-handed pianist, his medley of songs of the civil war brought the crowd repeatedly to its feet.

In a finale dramatic for its very understatement, the Internationals were called on stage,

and each was handed a single, long-stemmed red carnation. They stood quietly, holding aloft their tiny rewards. One Lincoln was heard to say: "This is the second happiest day of my life. The first was the day I came to Spain."

The tour became a time of reflection. When La Pasionaria, a frail ninety-one, met with the Internationals, Jim Yates gently kissed her and said: "Pasionaria, we are here." Other vets told how moving it was to be in the presence of this symbol of Spain's resistance to fascism, who in 1938 had said, "Come back."

Memories of war returned—crawling over the Pyrenees, firing three bullets into a hill, and then facing Franco's regular army and the army of

Ed Balchowsky plays the piano.

Africa, the Nazi Condor Legion, two Portuguese divisions, and fifty thousand of Mussolini's best troops fresh from victory in Ethiopia. Talk was of fear and controlling it, of being bombed in hospitals, of buddies who died or were captured. Soldiers remembered battlefield longings—a shower, a delousing unit, decent coffee, American cigarettes, hot food, and leave in Madrid, an end to the fierce summer heat or piercing winter cold.

After Madrid, huge bus caravans sped off to formal ceremonies in Saragossa, Valencia, Caspé, Gandesa, and Barcelona. Their arrival often led to TV and front-page news coverage.

In tiny Caspé, the mayor asked Lincolns to help lay a wreath at their simple granite monument: a dove of peace and "Our Sons, 1936-1939." Californians Milton Wolff and Bill Bailey towered over the neatly dressed, dark-suited peasant men and women who waited to shake their hands.

The Fiftieth Anniversary Tour buttons and local TV coverage attracted attention. Some shopkeepers in Madrid and Barcelona refused to take the Americans' money and instead wanted to shake their hands. A Madrid subway teller waved a large group through without payment and hugged the last veteran. Young men and women in Madrid and Barcelona walked up to shake hands. A bank in Barcelona did not charge tour people an exchange fee. Hilda Roberts, Bill Bailey, and Harry Hakim spoke before a high school class of a war about which Franco's school system had taught little.

The tour was forever uncovering hidden excitement. At Montserrat Monastery, the abbot welcomed the Americans to a large library of civil war volumes. He proudly revealed that his monastery had defied Franco by providing sanctuary for hundreds of refugees. In Barcelona, the tour's women, who said they were unrepresented, organized a U.S.-Spanish feminist con-

Veteran Jim Yates stands before a Gandesa monument honoring the republic.

Milton Wolff meets ex-Republican soldiers from Caspé.

Peace March leaves New York's Central Park, 1982. *Left to right:* Jim Yates, Bill Van Felix, Moe Fishman

Vieques March, New York City, Fall 2000. Martin Balter (*left*) and Moe Fishman (*right*) carry the VALB Banner.

ference with fifteen Spanish women, tape recorders, and three translators.

At Valanueva Pardillo, overlooking a lovely green valley, the tour paid homage to Lincoln Commander Oliver Law, who had died there. With a soft breeze blowing his thinning hair, Steve Nelson reminded the assembled women and men: "This was a historic moment—a black man was placed in charge of a largely white unit for the first time in U.S. history." Referring to the estimated 120 blacks who served, he emphasized, "We were integrated from top to bottom, and we want the world to share in the pride that we all feel." Next to Nelson was Harry Fisher, seventy-five, who was with Law when he was mortally wounded leading his men.

When U.S. reporters asked if Communists organized the International Brigades, Charlie Nusser laughed and said he would have volunteered for Spain if "the czar of Russia directed recruiting." In a Barcelona rally he shouted, "The republic we fought for was betrayed by the U.S. government, which enforced the arms embargo and sold oil and trucks to Franco. With guns, damn it, we would have won!"

The strong beliefs that once drove them across the Atlantic and over the Pyrenees still powered them. "My months in Spain were worth more than all the rest," said Nusser, and others nodded. The first night in Madrid, some Lincolns heard of a workers' demonstration against a plant closing. Despite jet lag, men in their seventies charged out to pitch in. Seeing their buttons, the demonstrators hugged them and dragged them into the line of march.

In October, 1988, to commemorate the fiftieth annniversary of the day the International Brigades left Spain, hundreds of surviving members, their families, and friends, assembled in Barcelona for the dedication of a monument to the foreign volunteers crafted by U.S. artist Roy Shifrin. Republican veterans' associations arranged a ceremony attended by more than a thousand people, including 118 from the United States. VALB Commander Steve Nelson, one of two International Brigade speakers, was brief: "When the governments of the Western democracies chose to sit on their hands . . . it was the common people who . . . rushed to the aid of the republic and said, 'We are with you.' In the words of Ernest Hemingway, 'No man ever entered earth more honorably than those who died in Spain.'"

In 1995 the Spanish Parliament—including a few former Franco sympathizers—voted unanimously to grant citizenship to the 500 to 1000 surviving International Brigaders, and the government invited them to Spain the next year to celebrate the 60th anniversary of the crusade against fascism.

But after conservative Jose Maria Aznar narrowly defeated Socialist Felipe Gonzales for the presidency, no government funds were available. Then 100,000 Spanish citizens donated five to ten dollars each to insure the success of the planned *Homenaje*, or homage. Young students formed an "Asociacio'n de Amigos" to provide services for what turned out to be 380 veterans from 29 countries accompanied by almost five hundred family members.

The several hundred Americans formed the largest contingent.

The unanimous parliatmentary vote, the official invitation and the Amigos' youthful verve assured a groundswell of popular support. But first the *Homenaje* had to steer through murky waters. Despite President Aznar's promise to meet them, neither he nor his top aides were on

American artist Roy Shifrin's bronze monument, which depicts David defeating Goliath, dominates Barcelona's northeast entrance. In the foreground is teacher Tom Kozar, who is on a quest to unearth the full story of his father, John, a seaman and Lincoln Brigader, who survived Spain but died as a sailor on a U.S. merchant ship during World War II, before Tom was born.

hand. Citizenship was bestowed by "a minor official who perfunctorily handed over a packet of documents to a representative of each national delegation," wrote Milton Wolff, last commander of the Lincoln Brigade. However, Lincoln Brigaders could not accept Spanish citizenship without surrendering their U.S. citizenship.

More than 20 newspaper articles denounced Aznar's "failure of common courtesy," and extended the Brigaders a warm welcome, and one editor called them "self-sacrificing and generous men and women motivated by idealism [who] offered their lives for the Spanish Repub-

lic." Many became instant media stars, trailed by TV cameras and newspaper reporters. Interviews with Brigaders were reprinted in Italian, French and British papers.

For the Amigos and Amigas the *Homenaje* became a frantic 20-hour a day effort to solve travel problems, carry luggage, run errands, serve dinners, clear tables, and push wheelchairs. At the Jarama river where Lincolns first shed their blood for the Republic, more than 350 Brigaders touched, remembered, and cried together.

At Madrid's Sports Palace Bragidistas, Amigo Robert Coane reported, were escorted "through a sea of people who parted, applauding and cheering." Coane turned to see his group "teary-eyed and deeply touched as they were cheered, hugged, their hands shaken and their backs patted." Inside an audience of 10,000 sang Spanish Civil War war songs and roared greetings as crying veterans raised their fists in salute.

In Barcelona's railroad station Brigaders arrived to a recording of La Passionaria's last speech and to see red, anarchist, Republican and Catalan flags move "like waves in an ocean of color, mingling with people of all ages and nationalities," reported Professor Vicente Navarro who stood in the crowd. Veteran James Benet and his wife walked "between the roped-back crowds cheering us and clapping" toward "a brass band playing old wartime tunes."

At the Catalan Parliament the next day Benet saw that "huge flag-waving crowds lined the long driveway and some of them had climbed into trees, just as American kids would do, waving and shouting." At Barcelona's Palace of Sports Bob Reed's wheel-chair was pushed through "a mass of cheering people on both sides. My lap was covered with flowers, presents and printed material from unions and other organizations." He cried as people hugged and kissed him and he said, "I couldn't grasp all the offered hands and there were many pats on the

Holding aloft their banner at the base of the Barcelona monument are Lincoln Brigaders (*left to right*) Morris Brier, Saul Wellman, Steve Nelson, Blas Padrino (Cuban), Bill Van Felix, and Gerald Glow (Canadian).

head from people I could not see."

In cities and small towns trade unionists and citizens turned out to thank men and women who had stood with them. In Albacete, where Lincolns trained for battle in 1937, the mayor, university and government officials ushered them into a museum dedicated to the International Brigades. The mayor told Benet and others they were "Spanish, now and in history."

At the Seville rail station the family of veteran Archie Brown arrived to find thousands of people. "We were inundated by waves of roaring sound, expressing their love and thanks for the Vets," reported Brown's daughter Susheela. "I will never forget this incredible sharing of emotion."

In the tiny town of Madrigueras sixty years earlier Harry Fisher had been adopted by a Spanish family. This time everyone wanted to adopt him, his children and grandchildren. As the Fishers left, "young people lined the street and stood silently with clenched fist salutes," and "older women began running along the side of my car, crying and throwing kisses." For Fisher it recalled an early dawn when he left Madrigueras in 1937 for the front and "the whole town had surrounded our two trucks, giving us food, and cry-

ing as we headed off. Then, too, many had silently raised their clenched fists in salute."

In Alcorcon, a Madrid suburb, Fisher and his family arrived to "a school yard filled with children waving and smiling." They were led to a feast, then to a gym crammed with high school students, and one thanked them "for helping their ancestors fight against the fascists." Alcorcon's Mayor welcomed Milton Wolff and Harry Fisher, and citizens came bearing "bouquets and medals," Wolff wrote. For him Alcorcon was the highlight of the trip: "We really got close to the people, where we experienced an exchange of love and respect, and admiration that was truly mutual. Come back they said, as Dolores had bid us do sixty years before. We were back, and we will come back again."

Lincolns often stumbled into the unexpected. David Smith met a German woman surgeon who had served in war with her surgeon husband. As they talked Smith realized it was her husband, along with a British surgeon, "who had operated on me at the hospital in Mataro. Much hugging followed."

At Hill 666, where Lincolns died in 1938, Milton Wolff remembered a senseless attack that

took many lives, "the cavalry assault on our hill," and a night encounter that led to the loss of dear friends. Fisher had "terrible memories": a friend blown twenty feet into the air, another who "lost both his eyes," and another severely wounded but "refusing help until others whom he considered more seriously wounded could be attended to." Eunice Lipton visited Hill 666 where her uncle Dave died before she was born. She "went to Spain out of respect and longing. I met wonderful vets and their partners and friends. I walked the streets of Madrid and stared at bullet-strafed buildings. I listened rapt and heartbroken to the *Internationale*."

"Never in recent history have Spaniards displayed such an outpouring of love and emotion for a group of people as they did for the Brigadistas," Professor Navarro wrote. Bob Reed felt the homage "was the most meaningful experience of my life." Pascual Maragall, Mayor of Barcelona, summarized the *Homenaje*: "The Brigadistas were the best that the twentieth century had offered. Their sense of committment and selflessness have been an inspiration to all freedom fighters in the world."

By 2000, International Brigade memorials stood in France, China, Germany, Poland, Italy, Luxembourg, Switzerland, Ireland, England, Cuba, Austrialia, Scotland, and Canada. In Chicago in 1989, Mayor Harold Washington proclaimed a day to honor the Lincoln Brigade and Commander Oliver Law. In the l930s Law had been jailed and beaten by Chicago police for speaking for the unemployed. Other memorials were planned.

Today the men and women of the Lincoln Brigade stand tall. They sounded the first alarm, and though poorly trained and underequipped, they stood up to world fascism. Theirs was also the first effort to knit together people from every corner of the globe into a Grand Alliance against Hitler and Mussolini. In less than a decade they joined a United Nations that was finally able to destroy the Axis Powers.

The surviving men and women of the Lincoln Brigade never stopped fighting. They returned from Spain to struggle for civil rights, civil liberties and against U.S. intervention abroad. With their energy, valor and optimism, they won and lost some battles and paid a terrible cost. They also shaped America's protest tradition and wrote a proud chapter in the history of world freedom.

(*Left*) Lincoln Brigade parades through Alcala de Henaren, May 1, 1937.

Annotated Bibliography

Bessie, Alvah. *Men in Battle* [San Francisco, 1975]

Carroll, Peter. *The Odessey of the Abraham Lincoln Brigade* [Stanford, 1994]

Colodny, Robert G. *The Struggle for Madrid: The Central Epic of the Spanish Conflict* [New York, 1958]

Fisher, Harry. *Comrades:Tales of a Bragadista in the Spanish Civil War* [Lincoln, 1998]

Geiser, Carl. *Prisoners of The Good Fight* [Westport, 1986]

Jackson, Gabriel. *The Spanish Republic and the Civil War*, 1931-1939 [Princeton, 1965]

Landis, Arthur. *The Abraham Lincoln Brigade* [New York, 1967]

Nelson, Carey, and Jefferson Hendricks, *Madrid 1937: Letters of the Abraham Lincoln Brigade from the Spanish Civil War* [New York, 1996]

Nelson, Steve. *The Volunteers* [New York, 1953]

Rolfe, Edwin. *The Lincoln Battalion* [New York, 1939]

Thomas, Hugh. *The Spanish Civil War* [New York, 1961]

Yates, James. *Mississippi to Madrid: Memoires of a Black American in the Spanish Civil War, 1936-1938* [Seattle,1988]

Wolff, Milton. *Another Hill* [Urbana, 1994]

Index